Presented To:

_____

From:

_____

Date:

_____

Define Your
DESTINY
through PRAYER

DESTINY IMAGE BOOKS BY SUE CURRAN

Prayer in Another Dimension

Define Your
DESTINY
through PRAYER

Your Journey
to
Divine Revelation

Sue Curran

DESTINY IMAGE® PUBLISHERS, INC.
P.O. Box 310, Shippensburg, PA 17257-0310
"Promoting Inspired Lives."

This book and all other Destiny Image, Revival Press, MercyPlace, Fresh Bread, Destiny Image Fiction, and Treasure House books are available at Christian bookstores and distributors worldwide.

For a U.S. bookstore nearest you, call 1-800-722-6774.
For more information on foreign distributors, call 717-532-3040.
Reach us on the Internet: www.destinyimage.com.

ISBN 13 TP: 978-0-7684-0281-0
ISBN 13 Ebook: 978-0-7684-8808-1

For Worldwide Distribution, Printed in the U.S.A.

1 2 3 4 5 6 7 8 / 16 15 14 13 12

DEDICATION

Two of my greatest mentors have gone on to their reward in heaven. Dr. Judson Cornwall, my pastor for thirty-one years, and Dr. Fuchsia Pickett, my dear friend and colleague, walked out their lives before me in such a way that I understood what true fathers and mothers in the faith should be.

This book is dedicated to them with grateful and loving memories for the mark they both left on my life. The journey that God set for me required strong and faithful support and leadership from those who had travelled this way before me.

ENDORSEMENTS

It is a delight to recommend Sue's book, *Define Your Destiny Through Prayer*. Sue is an amazing woman of God, who walks closely with the Holy Spirit. Her hunger for God's presence and her desire for deep intimacy with Jesus flows through every page of this book. Sue's personal journey of worship and prayer will challenge and encourage you to press in to your own encounters with Jesus.

I pray that as you read this book the Holy Spirit ignites your heart with greater passion and intimacy with Jesus and that you begin to bear exponential fruit all year round!

HEIDI BAKER, PhD
Founding Director, Iris Global

Define Your Destiny Through Prayer is a wonderful book, filled with inspiration and insight. Any time I have the privilege of reading about the journey of a seasoned prayer warrior like Dr. Sue Curran, I have the feeling I'm standing on holy ground. That is exactly what I felt with this book. Her quest for the heart of God is striking. It's hard to read this book and remain unchanged. Sue's story and insights will challenge every reader, as she gives us a glimpse into her intimate relationship with the Holy Spirit, presented in an accessible way. Readers will discover a practical and clear roadmap of how to begin to trust and hear the Holy Spirit for themselves. I highly recommend this book.

BILL JOHNSON
Bethel Church, Redding, California
Author, *When Heaven Invades Earth* and *Face to Face with God*

In her new book, Dr. Sue Curran x-rays our prayer lives and skillfully helps us identify and remove the obstacles.

Then, like a surgeon, she inserts the stints that reopen the life-giving flow of successful communication with the Holy Spirit.

JOHN KILPATRICK
Pastor, Church of His Presence
Daphne, Alabama

I am happy to recommend this book because it will inspire your own journey of vision and completion of what you are called to fulfill. Dr. Sue Curran takes you through the growing pains of learning how to pray by the leadership of the Holy Spirit. You will learn how to allow the Holy Spirit to speak through you the building blocks of success. Some of us put off praying due to lack of understanding of the ministry of the Holy Spirit. This book is not theory or just theology but an actual experiencing the reality of birthing the ministry that has come to be known as Shekinah. You too will be encouraged to see yourself growing as you read this spectacular account. I remember when the Lord gave me a prophetic word for Shekinah and it is exciting to see it threaded throughout this book.

Those who read this chronicle of Shekinah will develop a greater intimacy with Jesus and fellowship with the Holy Spirit.

KERRY KIRKWOOD
Senior Pastor, Trinity Fellowship
East Tyler, Texas

CONTENTS

FOREWORD

SUE CURRAN DOES IT AGAIN! This erudite, eloquent, and immensely thought-provoking work gets to the heart of the deepest passions and aspirations of the human heart, getting prayer answered.

This is indispensable reading for anyone who wants to live life above the norm and experience the exceptional prayer life . This is a profound authoritative work which spans the wisdom of the ages and yet breaks new ground in its approach and will possibly become a classic in this and the next generation.

This exceptional work by Dr. Sue Curran is one of the most profound, practical, principle-centered approaches to this subject of prayer I have read in a long time. The author's approach to this timely issue brings a fresh breath of air that captivates the heart, engages the mind and inspires the spirit of the reader.

The author's ability to leap over complicated theological and metaphysical jargon and reduce complex theories to simple practical principles that the least among us can understand is amazing.

This work will challenge the intellectual while embracing the laymen as it dismantles the mysterious of the soul search of mankind and delivers the profound in simplicity on the subject on Prayer.

Dr. Curran's approach awakens in the reader the untapped inhibiters that retard our personal development and her antidotes empower us to rise above these self-defeating, self-limiting factors to a life of exploits in spiritual and mental advancement in the area of effective prayer.

The author also integrates into each chapter the time-tested precepts giving each principle a practical application to life, making the entire process people-friendly.

Every sentence of this book is pregnant with wisdom and I enjoyed the mind-expanding experience of this exciting book. I admonish you to plunge into this ocean of knowledge and watch your life change for the better.

DR. MYLES MUNROE
BFM International
ITWLA
Nassau, Bahamas

INTRODUCTION

PRAYER DOES NOT HAVE TO BE a jungle of confusion. Neither does God intend for it to be difficult and beyond our reach. In fact, one of the important reasons He gave us the Holy Spirit is to help us pray. The Scriptures promise that He will dwell in believers and pray through us.

God called me into ministry immediately when He saved me. Early in my Christian life, He gave me a vision so expansive that it could only be accomplished through consistent, clear communication with Him to receive the direction and empowerment that was needed to fulfill it. As I sought to obey Him, to walk out what He showed me I should do for His name and glory, I developed an intimate relationship with Him in prayer.

Through this prayer lifestyle I learned that if I would call, He would answer (see Ps. 91:15). The vision God gave me involved establishing a conference and training center on a 160-acre campus. From the very beginning, I was pressed into discovering the path of prayer that would result in actually receiving answers for seemingly impossible goals.

You see, I understood that I was really in over my head. In order to succeed, I had to find out how to receive miracles that would create "something out of nothing." The Holy Spirit came to my rescue. He taught me how to pray. He showed me how He would pray through me.

In my growing dependency on Him, He ushered me into a spiritual realm of being led and empowered by the gifts of the Spirit. He showed me how these gifts should be used to help me pray effectively.

It is natural for us to think that we should pray from our thoughts and be guided by our own wisdom. But God is Spirit, and we must connect with His wisdom through our born-again spirits, which are indwelt by the Holy Spirit. In this divine relationship, He has provided the means for us to pray prayers that are according to His desire and purpose. That is why it is imperative that we surrender ourselves to be His instruments of prayer. We must allow the Holy Spirit to teach us to pray.

During the last four decades, as I have traveled throughout our nation and many others in ministry, I have become aware that there are many who really are yearning to have an effective prayer life. They have a desire for a personal relationship with Jesus that is at the same time intimate and powerful so that they can please God in their prayers.

Most believers understand that the Word of God teaches that the purpose of prayer is to receive answers. Yet, their seeming lack of effectiveness has left them discouraged and asking the question, "What more can I do to be a person whose prayers are answered?"

I invite you to come with me as I retrace the steps of my journey that established me in a lifestyle of effectual prayer. Born out of a growing intimacy with Jesus Christ, my prayer life was the catalyst that thrust me into the fulfillment of His mandate on my life. The Holy Spirit taught me to pray according to the will of God. He is available to every believer, and He wants to reveal Jesus to you, lead you into all truth, and give you a powerful, effective, and productive life of prayer.

It seems God is limited by our prayer life—that He can do nothing for humanity unless someone asks Him.

—John Wesley[1]

HAVING TROUBLE PRAYING?

As a pastor, I understand that many people have problems cultivating an effective prayer life. And I believe, in their minds, those problems are real. Some sincere, born-again Christians say, "I don't know how to begin. Can I really learn to pray?"

Others admit, "I feel awkward speaking to someone I can't see, like I'm just putting words into the air. What should I say? Will God really hear me?"

Still others feel, "I'm not good enough to pray." Unfortunately, there are also Christians who simply feel that prayer is boring.

You may desire to experience fellowship with God through prayer. However, because of these or other struggles, that desire may seem hopelessly out of reach for you. You may even wonder if intimate, divine relationship with God through prayer is real. Perhaps you reason that if it is, maybe it is just for a "gifted" few who are privileged to know how to pray.

I often hear such expressions of frustration from believers who have not "figured out" their own practical involvement in prayer. I am aware that often our enemy, the devil, enters this arena gleefully to aggravate a believer's "mind battle" regarding prayer. He tries to persuade a person that pursuing a life of prayer is not really worth the effort. He may suggest subtly that, "It probably isn't doing much good anyway."

However, the truth is that if you don't develop a robust prayer life, it is inevitable that your Christian walk will suffer debilitation and a sense of powerlessness. Your half-hearted attempts to pray may seem so futile that you are tempted to give it up altogether. If that is true for you, these unresolved struggles will ultimately rob you of the intimate relationship with God that He desires for you to enjoy.

GOOD NEWS!

I have good news for you. God never intended for you to have to work through these problems concerning prayer on your own. He doesn't expect you to "figure out" how to pray in order to succeed in enjoying communion with the Lord.

According to the Scriptures, God, the Father, sent Jesus to die for your sins and to reconcile you to Himself. When Jesus returned to the Father, He sent the Holy Spirit, the Third Person of the Trinity, to lead you into all truth (see John 16:13).

When you accepted Jesus as your Savior, God gave you the precious gift of His Holy Spirit. His express purpose for giving you the Holy Spirit was to help you resolve all of life's issues, including your issues with your prayer life. One of the Holy Spirit's assignments in your life is to teach you to pray:

> *And the Holy Spirit helps us in our distress. For we don't even know what we should pray for, nor how we should pray. But the Holy Spirit prays for us with groanings that cannot be expressed in words. And the Father who knows all hearts knows what the Spirit is saying, for the Spirit pleads for us believers in harmony with God's own will* (Romans 8:26-27 NLT).

BEGINNING MY JOURNEY INTO PRAYER

Looking back over my Christian life, I realize that I learned to pray early in my ministry because I desperately needed God's help for what

He had called me to do. On that memorable day in 1967, when I gave my heart to Jesus Christ, He startled me by calling me into ministry. God radically changed my career plans that day. Instinctively, I knew I needed God to give me faith for what He had called me to do. I understood that, for me, it was *learn to pray—or perish*. But, I am ahead of the story.

It all began when I married my high school sweetheart, John. Shortly after we were married, John enlisted in the U.S. Army. I remember the day when he came home on his first leave. We drove out to the lake and sat in the car, discussing our immediate future for several hours. We wanted so much to be together. But we realized that was not going to be feasible, financially.

John and I addressed the problem logically, calculating what it would cost for both of us to live at Fort Jackson in Columbia, South Carolina, where he was stationed. We wisely concluded that we could never make it on his pay as an Army Private, First Class. We convinced each other that the only sensible thing to do was me to stay in Kingsport, Tennessee, and for John to go back to Fort Jackson—alone.

"All right," I concurred, "then that's that."

John agreed, "It's the only thing that makes sense."

Having both accepted our "wise" decision, we drove home, packed all our earthly belongings (which wasn't much), put them into our little car, and drove together to Fort Jackson—that day.

Amazingly, we survived. We even saved enough money during the three years of his enlistment to pay for John's entire college education (before the GI Bill). After John's discharge from the Army, we returned home to Kingsport. I got a job as secretary to the president of a large local industry, and John entered college, studying to become a chemist.

We also began attending a large Methodist church in our city. My mother was an earnest Pentecostal believer. I had attended church with her as a child. She was a living witness to me of her fervent love for Jesus. Her life was a convincing testimony that she trusted the Lord and had committed her life to Him.

Still, I had never followed her example of commitment to the Lord by giving my heart to Jesus. I had actually determined to keep my distance from truly committed believers. In my heart, I knew I was not ready to "count the cost" as Jesus had taught we must do in order to follow Him (see Luke 14).

TAPPED FOR LEADERSHIP

In spite of the fact that we were not born-again Christians, my husband and I were asked to be youth leaders in our Methodist church. We accepted the opportunity to serve our church youth. For one of their activities, we took our group of eighty teens to a weekend retreat. As it turned out, we were being "set up" by the Holy Spirit, who was about to change all our lives—eternally.

Part of the program that weekend involved another group of young people giving their testimonies. They had recently accepted Christ as their personal Savior. Their radiant faces, youthful enthusiasm, and the joy they expressed at knowing that their sins were forgiven was mesmerizing. They shared how their lives were completely changed by simply receiving Jesus as their Savior. They declared their determination to commit their whole lives to Him to do His will. Their love for the Lord was intoxicating.

That weekend, many of our teens were inspired by these vibrant young Christians to surrender their lives to Jesus. And so were my husband and I! When I walked out the door of my cabin the next morning, I really was a "new creature." It seemed to me that God had painted the sky just for me. The dewdrops looked like diamonds sparkling in the grass. Nature all around me looked as washed and clean as I felt. It seemed like I had just stepped into a new world. In a very real way, I had done just that.

I remember hearing an old story of a revival where the preacher got saved. The people of the church were so excited that they ran from house to house exclaiming, "The parson got saved! The parson got saved!" Our Methodist youth were just as excited that John and I, their youth leaders, were experiencing that same reality of salvation along with them. It was a high moment in all of our lives.

Needless to say, we returned home with a "new" youth group. John and I were also new creatures in Christ, as the Scriptures say:

> *Therefore if any man be in Christ, he is a new creature: old things are passed away; behold, all things are become new* (2 Corinthians 5:17).

We knew we had been changed by the wonderful, saving grace of God. But we could not imagine how different our lives were to become, nor how soon it would begin to happen.

Our youth group now exuded the same joy and enthusiasm we had witnessed in the young people at the retreat who had given their testimonies. They could not wait to share their joyful experience of being born again. When we told our pastor what had happened at the retreat, he rejoiced with us. Then he gave the youth group the entire Sunday morning service to share their testimonies.

We watched in amazement as adults were moved to tears when they listened to these excited young people tell how they had met Jesus. And we were astounded to see the altar filled that morning with many people coming to receive salvation. Others came to ask God to touch their lives again with His presence.

Methodist churches in our area began to hear the news of the "revival" in our church (I didn't even know the term *revival* at the time). Pastors began to invite us to their churches to give our testimonies. For seventeen straight nights, we took our youth group to neighboring churches to share what Jesus had done for them.

Everywhere we went, many youth and adults were receiving salvation after hearing the joyful testimonies of our youth. Our entire city was buzzing with the news of this strange and wonderful thing that was happening as hundreds of people were finding Jesus as their personal Savior.

PRAY....SOMETHING!

With the altars of churches continually filling with people of all ages seeking to receive Jesus as their Savior, we were called upon to pray for them. But we had only been saved for a few weeks; we were not trained to lead someone to Christ. That was when I first realized I had to learn to pray—or perish!

As young people flooded the altars, they sobbed and cried out, "We want what you have. We want to know Jesus like you do!" Good. Wonderful. That is what we wanted for them. But they were expecting me to pray to help them receive Jesus as their Savior. I had no idea what to pray.

Then, in one church, where the altars once again filled with youth crying out to God, I looked around desperately for help. As I did, I noticed an elderly man praying and crying with the kids as they poured their hearts out to God. Later, I learned that he was a retired preacher who loved God and was thrilled with what was happening.

If I can just get over there beside him, I thought, *I can find out what to pray.* So I worked my way around the people at the altar to get to where he was praying with someone. I listened to what he prayed. His simple prayer went like this: "Lord, look in tender mercy on this one who has come to You tonight."

Ecstatic, I thought, *I can do this!* So, I practiced his prayer a few times to myself, *"Lord, look in tender mercy..."* I didn't know exactly what it meant, but I prayed those words sincerely for these young people, and they left the altar happy.

In spite of my ignorance, God did have mercy as He has promised to do for all who seek Him. His Word declares that "everyone who calls upon the name of the Lord will be saved" (Acts 2:21 NLT). Later I would understand that it was not a "prayer formula" that brought His salvation to their hearts; it was simply a genuine heart cry. I was learning to pray.

The Holy Spirit was moving so mightily in conviction on the hearts of these youth. I just needed to pray *something*—to acknowledge the mercy of God that was bringing them to salvation. That was my first lesson from the Holy Spirit teaching me to pray. I smile now remembering that I used a "borrowed prayer" from a godly preacher in my first lesson on prayer.

God was always faithful to send help to me exactly when I needed it. In those first years of my ministry, He led me to people who would teach me principles of obeying His Word. As I sought God, desiring to fulfill His purposes, He brought amazing people into my life who would mentor me, teaching me how to be led by the Spirit. And I would go anywhere I heard God was doing something wonderful in people's lives.

In fact, from the very beginning, this pattern for my future ministry was established. I would hear that God was doing wonderful things in a certain place, and I determined to find out for myself what He was doing. In time, I was traveling to different nations and continents to continue my lifelong pursuit of learning to live in the presence and power of God. But more about that later...

I ought to pray before seeing anyone. Christ arose before day and went into a solitary place. David says, "Early will I seek thee." I feel it is far better to begin with God – to see His face first, to get my soul near Him, before it is near another.

—Murray M'Cheyene[1]

Prayer—secret, fervent, believing prayer—lies at the root of all personal godliness.

—William Carey[2]

CHAPTER 2

A DEVOTIONAL PRAYER LIFESTYLE

MAYBE YOU JUST GET TIRED of hearing people talking about their relationships with Jesus in a way to which you cannot relate. When they use phrases like, "The Lord told me," or "The Holy Spirit showed me," or "God gave me a vision," perhaps you think, *What if someone would really explain how that happens? What does it mean? Do they literally "see" Him? Do they actually hear His voice?*

I remember feeling that way at times, especially when a trusted minister would begin to relate what sounded like a lengthy conversation he had with Jesus—you know, the kind that is complete with "He said" and "Then I said." Sometimes I didn't really believe people had these conversations with Jesus; rather, I thought perhaps they simply had a great imagination.

Certainly it is difficult to articulate spiritual experiences in human terms. Sometimes we simply receive an impression of what we should do. At other times, we receive ideas that we recognize are from God (i.e., they agree with His written Word). At times, we can actually converse with the Lord, asking questions and receiving His answers. However we experience it, the bottom line is that divine communication with God is real for the believer.

It is simply a wonderful reality that God does communicate personally with His children. How else do you explain, for example, the manifest peace and joy that people experience when they are born again? They *know* that God has received their request to receive His salvation; they know that their sins are forgiven. How was that "communicated" to their minds, their emotions?

It might be different for every person. It is often hard to describe in human language. The fact is, some of the most powerful communications we receive come to us without words. But the end result is the same: We know that we know.

Early in my Christian life, I found that the essential key to communing and communicating with God is cultivating a devotional prayer lifestyle. That is, in order to learn to hear God's voice, you must get to know Him personally through private time that you spend with Him. One of many scriptural exhortations that reveals this prerequisite to knowing God is: "Be still, and know that I am God..." (Ps. 46:10).

CULTIVATING INTIMACY WITH GOD

Human relationship in its essence is a two-way street. It requires communication—speaking and listening—in order to develop a healthy interaction with one you love. Similarly, through devotional prayer, which involves both speaking and listening, you cultivate an interactive relationship with God. You speak to Him, and then you wait expectantly for Him to speak to you.

From the outset of my walk with God, I began to cultivate a devotional time each morning. It was time I spent alone with the Word of God and talking with the Lord. The Holy Spirit led me to read Scriptures that showed me His way to establish a relationship with Him. I began to understand that intimacy with God doesn't happen just because we are saved; it is a result of pursuing Him on a daily basis.

I saw in the Scriptures that David, the psalmist, who really knew God, mentioned consistent times every day for prayer and worship: "Evening, and morning, and at noon, will I pray, and cry aloud: and he shall hear my voice" (Ps. 55:17). And I was fascinated with the concept

I read over and over in the Psalms—which at the time I little understood—seeking the Lord.

In fact, throughout the Old and New Testaments, this concept of seeking the Lord is emphasized by Moses, by all of the prophets, and by Jesus Himself. Jeremiah declares this wonderful promise of God: "And ye shall seek me, and find me, when ye shall search for me with all your heart" (Jer. 29:13). The very next verse emphasizes the result: "And I will be found of you..." (Jer. 29:14). It soon became clear to me from many such Scriptures that God expects us to seek Him.

Another part of the biblical pattern I discovered for cultivating a devotional prayer lifestyle was making it daily—"morning by morning." The prophet Isaiah declared: "...he wakeneth morning by morning, he wakeneth mine ear to hear as the learned" (Isa. 50:4).

The Holy Spirit showed me that the fruit of my lips was pleasing to Him:

> *Take with you words, and turn to the Lord: say unto him, Take away all iniquity, and receive us graciously: so we will render the calves of our lips* (Hosea 14:2).

> *By him therefore let us offer the sacrifice of praise to God continually, that is, the fruit of our lips giving thanks to his name* (Hebrews 13:15).

So, I began to offer Him the first fruits of each day, the fruit of my lips. In time, I combined these biblical instructions and practiced them consistently to cultivate a devotional lifestyle and commune with the Lord:

> Come before Him every morning. Begin to worship Him by bringing words. Let them be the first words of the day. Humble yourself to seek His forgiveness. Ask and expect Him to open your ear to hear His voice. This is the pathway to divine communion.

If I did not start my day that way—every day—I was the loser. I learned not to wait until later in the day. It doesn't work. Simply put, the best time for morning prayer is in the morning. I often declare the words of the prophet Isaiah to express my expectation of hearing from the Lord daily:

> *The Lord God has given me the tongue of the learned, that I should know how to speak a word in season to him who is weary. He awakens me morning by morning. He awakens my ear to hear as the learned. The Lord God has opened my ear; and I was not rebellious...* (Isaiah 50:4-5 NKJV).

These verses are part of a messianic prophecy that revealed how Jesus would walk on the earth. He lived in total dependence upon His personal communion with the Father for all He said and did. Jesus confirmed this divine dependency on the Father in His own words:

> *Most assuredly, I say to you, the Son can do nothing of Himself, but what He sees the Father do; for whatever He does, the Son also does in like manner... I do not seek my own will but the will of the Father who sent me* (John 5:19,30 NKJV).

Jesus declared that He has sent us into the world as the Father sent Him into the world (see John 20:21). Dependency upon the Father was at the core of Jesus' relationship with Him. And that same dependency is the essence of our relationship with the Lord. It requires us to have our ears "awakened" to hear His voice. There is no sweeter sound than the voice of the Lord to satisfy the longing of the human heart. That heart-reality of knowing you have heard the loving voice of your Savior fills you with longing to continually know Him more.

"THERE I WILL GIVE YOU MY LOVES"

My desire every morning in spending time alone with the Lord is to hear His voice of love to me. Sometimes He causes a verse or passage out of His written Word to come alive to me. It will be revealed to me as I have never seen it before; it brings fresh faith or desire to my heart. At other times, His voice will simply be an impression in my spirit of what I should or should not do. Sometimes it brings a comforting presence of simply feeling loved and accepted in the beloved.

And sometimes He speaks words to me that I hear in my spirit. He has given me specific instructions regarding the vision that would become a reality as I obeyed His words to me. Each time I open my heart and bring my whole life to Him, I trust that the time I spend with Him is digging out a greater capacity to hear clearly from Him and be directed by His Spirit.

A few years ago, after living this lifestyle of devotional prayer for several decades, the Lord gave us an opportunity to reap a wonderful harvest of souls in the Ukraine. It was shortly after the collapse of the former Soviet Union, and I was preparing to take a team from our church to go to...I wasn't really sure where. I was working only with an interpreter from the Ukraine who had been recommended to us. No Ukrainian church or other local organization was hosting us. We were going in simple faith to touch the Ukrainian people, with great desire to be used by God to bring in this harvest.

During that first trip to the Ukraine, multiplied doors opened to us to share the gospel. Our youth sang choruses of praise in the Ukrainian language and performed heart-throbbing mimes, captivating to young and old alike. I preached the simple gospel message that was interpreted into their language. During ten days, over three thousand people accepted Christ as Savior.

I wept also as I realized that this wonderful harvest of souls had been birthed in my morning devotional prayer time. For over twenty-five years, I had cultivated my morning devotional time with the Lord. Now, as I waited before Him, He opened my eyes in a new way to the now familiar verses of the Song of Solomon:

> *I am my beloved's, and his desire is toward me. Come, my beloved, let us go forth into the field; let us lodge in the villages. Let us get up early to the vineyards; let us see if the vine flourish, whether the tender grape appear, and the pomegranates bud forth: there will I give thee my loves* (Song of Solomon 7:10-12).

As I read those words, my heart burned with desire to do just that, to see the tender young life of the precious Ukrainian people who had so long been deprived of the Word of Life. As a result, I pursued the arduous task of leading a team into that "field." I am so glad I did.

Once we are secure in our relationship with Jesus, our Beloved, and we know that "His desire is toward us," we have the confidence to answer His call to the harvest. In that intimate relationship, we come to realize we truly are co-laborers with Him as He extends the invitation to us to go with Him into the harvest.

I understood that ministry in the Ukraine would be to "the tender grapes that were just appearing," the fresh fields of the harvest. The added wonder of that promise to me was expressed in the words, "there I will give thee my loves" (Song of Sol. 7:12). Not only did we have the privilege of winning many souls to Jesus during those ten days, but I also experienced a greater capacity for trust and for personal relationship with Him than ever before. I touched the heart of God in His compassion for the Ukrainian people; I shall never forget it.

After what seemed like a lifetime of waiting on God, I was learning on a new level that all true kingdom fruit comes out of intimate relationship with the Lord. My relationship with God, which had been established through devotional prayer every morning of my life, helped me to hear clearly the voice of the Lord sending me now into the harvest. As in the natural, so in the spiritual, it is the intimacy of love that conceives and produces "fruit." Without that divine love relationship, there will be no spiritual fruit.

LOVE—NOT RULES

Some people feel guilty for not spending time with the Lord alone. Their mornings are too hectic; they are tired at night. Family places demands on them, and so forth. For many, this "legal" obligation to develop a devotional prayer life causes them to live in condemnation. Yet condemnation does not motivate them to change; it only makes them miserable when the subject is brought up.

Love, not rules, motivates you to wait on the Lord. When you are in love, you feel no obligation to find time to be with your beloved. That is where you want to be. When you become aware of how much Jesus loves you, it will not be difficult to devote time alone to be with Him. Jesus made it clear that He wants to have fellowship with you in order to love you and guide you into all truth:

> *If anyone loves Me, he will keep My word: and My Father will love him, and We will come to him; and make Our home with him. . . .The Helper, the Holy Spirit, whom the Father will send in My name, He will teach you all things and bring to your remembrance all things that I said to you* (John 14:23,26 NKJV).

Jesus has promised in His Word that intimate knowing of Him is His will and plan for all believers. So it should not be difficult to learn how to commune with Him. He wants you to allow the Holy Spirit to teach you. When you grasp the reality of God's love for you and *His* desire to commune with *you,* your only proper response is to say, *"Awesome!"*

God's plan is to make His home with you. Jesus said that those who love Him will be loved by His Father: "...and I will love him and manifest Myself to him" (John 14:21 NKJV). To manifest means "to show or demonstrate plainly, reveal, to be clearly apparent to the sight or understanding; obvious."[3]

There's no mystery here, no foggy notion or active imagination. God wants to communicate with you and let you share life with Him. It may not be possible at first for your mind to understand the depths of intimate relationship Jesus desires to have with you. That, too, is a work of the Holy Spirit.

INTIMACY SIMPLY KNOWS

When you enjoy intimate relationship with a person, you spontaneously communicate with that person in many ways. If you need help or just want that person to do something with you, it is just a matter of asking. When your heart overflows with admiration and devotion toward that person, you simply express your sheer delight with loving words of praise.

When you are hurting or frightened, you don't hesitate to cry on the shoulder of real friends and family; you know they expect you to "unload" on them. And if these relationships are threatened, you immediately challenge the enemy and stand against anything that would bring about their demise.

Similarly, when you walk in a lifestyle of intimate relationship with the Lord, you simply know how to communicate with Him. We call our communication with God *prayer* and classify various "kinds" of praying. For example, you are praying a *petition* prayer when you ask Him for something. You are *praising* God when you express your love and devotion; you are worshiping God when you pour out your heart to Him in response to His presence. And you are engaging in *spiritual warfare* when you challenge your enemies in the name of Jesus.

The more you read the Word of God and spend time waiting on Him, the more you will know that you are praying (communicating) according to His will. As you develop a personal devotional life with the Lord, the Holy Spirit will lead you into the depths of His love and show you His truth as it applies to your life. The heart satisfaction you discover there will propel you into an ever-deeper friendship with God.

FRIENDS WITH JESUS

In reality, it is quite simple to develop a devotional relationship with the Lord. The problems we have with devotional prayer can be overcome when we simply make a decision, in faith, to come to God as a little child. We must decide to open our lives to Him, determined to love Him and believing that He loves us back. Faith will fill our hearts as we meditate on His Word, which reveals His great love for us and His desire for us to abide in Him. We will experience the reality of His promise to make His abode in us:

Jesus answered and said unto him, If a man love me, he will keep my words: and my Father will love him, and we will come unto him, and make our abode with him (John 14:23).

I have chosen to embrace these words of Jesus, which promise that the Father and Jesus will make their home with all who love Him and obey His Word. Jesus calls you a "friend" rather than a servant because, He said, "all things that I heard from my Father I have made known unto you" (John 15:15). Servants don't know their master's plans or desires. Jesus wants to confide in you as His friend.

As in any relationship, it is necessary to find words to express your desires, your love, and your needs. They don't have to be eloquent words. They just need to be real and from your heart. As in any relationship, you also need to learn to listen, to hear what the Holy Spirit is saying to you in that moment. It may be from the written Word; it may come as an impression or idea; it may simply be a wonderful sense of His love and presence.

During my devotional time, I do not pray for people, seek direction for the church, or intercede for nations. This is my time with Him; it is His time with me. I settle in to talk to my Friend. I ask Him to speak to me. I open my life for His direction, correction, and instruction. Above all else, I give Him my praise, and I worship Him in deep gratitude for who He is.

Sometimes I say to the Lord: "I bring the first-fruits of this day to you. The fruit of my lips I offer to you" (see Hos. 14:2). I acknowledge that He alone is worthy of my worship. I tell Him simply, affectionately, that I love Him.

It is always good, especially when learning to express our love to Him, to use biblical expressions of adoration. The book of Psalms is filled with praise and worship language that teaches us to express the greatness of God and our gratitude for His love.

As you read the Scriptures, make it a point to note instances where people worshiped God and expressed their adoration for Him. Read those passages aloud and learn to quote them as a love expression from your own heart. For example, I love to worship the Lord with these words of adoration:

> *As the apple tree among the trees of the wood, so is my beloved among the sons. I sat down under his shadow with great delight, and his fruit was sweet to my taste* (Song of Solomon 2:3).

Your life will be forever transformed when you take the initiative to cultivate a devotional life with the Lord. I believe that in eternity we will simply continue what we began here—to know the Lord more intimately and to experience His love more deeply. For now, I can only imagine...

You and I must learn to pray from the river within us—not from the neck up, and not from the lips. We've got to get down deep into the river.

—Oral Roberts[1]

CHAPTER 3

SALVATION IS WONDERFUL…
BUT THERE'S MORE!

TWO YEARS AFTER I RECEIVED Jesus as my Savior, I was once again attending a Methodist retreat. And once again, I experienced another life-changing encounter with God. The Methodist preacher leading the retreat was teaching about the baptism of the Holy Spirit. He taught how early Christians received another experience of power after they had given their lives to Jesus (see Acts 1:5; 2:4; 10:47).

When he prayed for me, I gladly received the baptism of the Holy Spirit. This experience opened another dimension of prayer and of life in the Spirit to me. I felt as if I had literally walked through a door into a new spiritual realm. Here I became aware of powerful, spiritual gifts (see 1 Cor. 12) through which the Holy Spirit worked supernaturally in people to do His work. Ultimately, I found that this dimension of prayer was a place of revelation of God's heart, a place where I received faith to fulfill the calling of God on my life.

My immediate response was joy—outrageous joy. I remember feeling a sense of sheer exhilaration when the minister prayed for me. The retreat was being held in a resort located on the top of a mountain; it was covered in deep snow. With abandon, I ran out of the lodge and rolled in the snow, making snow angels by sliding my arms and legs back and forth, laughing and praising God.

From that rather undignified position, looking at the mountaintops above me, I felt like it would be easy to just leap from one to another. I was well aware that I was a mere mortal being on earth, but I was also keenly aware in that moment that I had touched heaven. Filled with new joy and a child-like faith, I soon realized that this wonderful empowering of the Holy Spirit was a new beginning for me. It would usher me into a divine relationship with Him in prayer that taught me how to be led by Him for the rest of my life.

I have heard it said that some people should be locked up for four months after receiving the baptism of the Holy Spirit because their zeal is so overwhelming to others. I was one of those people. I was determined everybody was going to receive what I had received. I simply had no clue as to why they would not want to do so.

Now, over four decades after receiving the baptism of the Holy Spirit, I still have a hard time understanding why people would not want to open their hearts to this wonderful experience. It has been my joy to pray for many people to receive this empowering of the Holy Spirit.

PRAYING IN THE HOLY SPIRIT

The Holy Spirit continued to teach me to pray. Indeed, facing the unexpected challenges of the ministry to which He was leading me, I was afraid *not* to pray. I had no idea how to lead the revivals for which I had received invitations. In my desperation, all I knew to do was to wait on God in prayer. The devotional prayer lifestyle He led me into became as necessary to my spiritual life as breathing was to my physical life. And it is still the same today.

As I studied the Scriptures, I began to understand the instructions Jesus gave to His disciples just before He returned to His Father. He prepared them to receive the empowering they would need to establish His kingdom in the earth:

...wait for the promise of the Father, which, saith he, ye have heard of me. For John truly baptized with water; but ye shall be baptized with the Holy Ghost not many days hence...ye shall receive power, after that the Holy Ghost is come upon you: and ye shall be witnesses unto me both in Jerusalem, and in all Judaea, and in Samaria, and unto the uttermost part of the earth (Acts 1:4-5, 8).

The Scriptures record that 120 of Jesus' followers obeyed His instructions. They gathered together in an upper room to wait for the baptism of the Holy Ghost that He said would come. When the day of Pentecost came, Jesus' promise was fulfilled for them. They heard a sound from heaven like a mighty rushing wind, and they saw cloven tongues like fire that sat on each of them: "And they were all filled with the Holy Ghost, and began to speak with other tongues, as the Spirit gave them utterance" (Acts 2:4).

I am aware of the great divide between Christians who love God, but do not believe in speaking in tongues, and those who do speak in tongues. It is not my purpose here to provide an apologetic for the doctrine of tongues or to explain why millions of Christians today speak with tongues.

I simply want to say to you that when I received the baptism of the Holy Spirit, I spoke in tongues. The supernatural prayer language I received in that wondrous experience filled me with love and joy. I expressed praise and worship to God in a satisfying way that I had not experienced before. Later, I found that I had a greater sensitivity to hear what the Holy Spirit was saying to me through the Word of God or in the still small voice in my heart.

Through the baptism of the Holy Spirit, I was ushered into a spiritual realm where the gifts of the Spirit were available to work in my life. These supernatural gifts provided the wisdom, knowledge, and divine direction that we needed to accomplish the work God had given us to do.

THE BIBLICAL BASIS FOR TONGUES

As a novice to the whole idea of tongues, I searched the Scriptures and found that speaking in tongues was most often the evidence of having received the baptism of the Holy Ghost (see Acts 2:4; 10:46; 8:16-17; 19:6). For example, when the God-fearing Gentile, Cornelius, asked Peter to come to him, Peter obeyed God's instructions to go. And when he preached the good news of the gospel of Christ to those who had gathered there, "the Holy Ghost fell on all them which heard the word...for they heard them speak with tongues, and magnify God" (Acts 10:44,46).

The apostle Paul explains that when you pray in tongues, you don't understand what you are saying, but in the spirit you are speaking mysteries to God (see 1 Cor. 14:2). While it is humbling to the intellect to utter words that you do not understand, your spirit is enthralled with the divine love that you are experiencing as you "speak mysteries" unto God:

> *For he that speaketh in an unknown tongue speaketh not unto men, but unto God: for no man understandeth him; howbeit in the spirit he speaketh myster-ies* (1 Corinthians 14:2).

The apostle Paul was a very educated man, highly regarded for his intellect and great learning. Yet Paul received the baptism of the Holy Spirit and spoke a language his mind did not understand. And he taught believers how to function in this divine gift:

> *What is it then? I will pray with the spirit, and I will pray with the under-standing also: I will sing with the spirit, and I will sing with the understanding also* (1 Corinthians 14:15).

I was learning that praying in the Spirit is a divine ability given specifically for communication between your spirit and God, who is spirit. Have you ever considered the wisdom of God in giving us a prayer language that the devil cannot understand? I don't blame the devil for resisting this gift and creating confusion in believers' minds to keep them from receiving it in faith. He cannot compete with our own love language that speaks mysteries unto God.

WORLD-WIDE OUTPOURING

Besides the Scriptures, I studied Church history and found that God had poured out His Spirit mightily around the turn of the twentieth century. People had received the baptism of the Holy Spirit around the world simultaneously. The gifts of the Spirit were manifest in all manner of healings and miracles, along with transformed lives and communities.

I researched the Azusa Street revival of Los Angeles, Maria Woodworth Etter's remarkable ministry of healing, Smith Wigglesworth, and scores of other ministers who embraced this "Pentecostal experience." Churches have been established in the last one hundred years in many nations that accept the biblical phenomena of spiritual gifts, including miracles, faith, healing, and speaking in tongues. Many of these Christians have received supernatural power to renounce false religions and endure terrible persecution from family, friends, and even governments.

David Yonggi Cho, founder of the largest church in the world in Seoul, South Korea, embraced the baptism of the Holy Spirit. He and his congregation have established a wonderful retreat center called Prayer Mountain. People come from around the world to fast and pray and wait on God alone in tiny grottoes for days or weeks at a time. There are as many as 25,000 people praying on that mountain every day. Prayer has been rising to God in this way for over twenty-five years.

Another example we witnessed in India are the thousands of Pentecostal Christians in the churches where we have ministered. In spite of the terrible persecution from those who worship false gods, these believers persevere in the love and power of God, winning others to the gospel of Jesus as well.

Among the countless churches that have embraced the gifts of the Spirit, testimonies of miracles of healing, deliverance, and even raising the dead abound. I believe it is the proper functioning of these super-natural power gifts that the Church needs today to conquer the terrible onslaught of the evil one against our lives, our families, our churches, and our communities.

THE HOLY SPIRIT HELPS US PRAY

Much of the praying we do in our own effort is intellectual. That is, we try to organize ideas in our minds and say them to God. We are not necessarily sensing the burden of the Lord or understanding what His will is for a given situation.

God knows we need help—first, to pray His will, and second, to be empowered to pray when we don't feel like it. These are two of the main reasons why He baptizes us with the Holy Spirit. He knows how much we need help to pray. We saw earlier in Romans 8:26 that when we are praying in the Spirit, He intercedes for us according to the will of God.

As the Third Person of the Godhead, who indwells you, He knows the will of God when you don't. And He will pray God's will through you when you pray in the Spirit. As you pray in tongues, you may not know in the moment what you have asked. But you do know that you have prayed the will of God, speaking mysteries to Him (see 1 Cor. 14:2). And in time, you will see the hand of God at work in your life situations. Your testimony confirms that God heard the cry of the Spirit as He prayed through you.

The times when you are too discouraged or weary to pray, I suggest that you begin to pray in tongues. According to the Scriptures, the Holy Spirit strengthens your faith to pray: "But ye, beloved, building up yourselves on your most holy faith, praying in the Holy Ghost (Jude 1:20).

As you are strengthened in your spirit—your inner self—faith rises, and you can overcome your lack of desire or any other distraction that keeps you from praying. Just knowing that the Holy Spirit is always praying the will of God and that His prayers will be answered encourages the heart. His supernatural power strengthens your entire person—body, mind, and spirit.

Learning about these two ministries of the Holy Spirit—that He helps me pray the will of God and that He strengthens my spiritual self—rescued me from thinking I always had to know how and what to pray. Learning to pray in the Spirit also delivered me from the struggle to "feel" or "faith" my way through difficult prayer times.

I finally got it. The Holy Spirit is the giver of prayers; He is the pray-er of prayers; He is the strengthener of my inner self. When I learn to yield to Him, He ends the struggle concerning prayer.

If you have not received the baptism of the Holy Ghost with the evidence of receiving a divine prayer language, it is available to you. In his sermon on the day of Pentecost, the apostle Peter indicated that there was no limit to those who could receive the gift of the Holy Ghost. The promise is to all who are called of God:

> *Then Peter said unto them, Repent, and be baptized every one of you in the name of Jesus Christ for the remission of sins, and ye shall receive the gift of the Holy Ghost. For the promise is unto you, and to your children, and to all that are afar off, even as many as the Lord our God shall call* (Acts 2:38-39).

Prayer is reaching out after the unseen; fasting is letting go of all that is seen and temporal. Fasting helps express, deepen, confirm the resolution that we are ready to sacrifice anything, even ourselves to attain what we seek for the kingdom of God.

—Andrew Murray[1]

CHAPTER 4

LEARNING TO FAST AND PRAY

BEFORE I KNEW THE MEANING of the word *mentor*, the Lord gave me one. Soon after my conversion experience, Venita Mack, an evangelist in the truest sense of that calling, became a spiritual mentor to me. Looking back, I realize that the Holy Spirit led me to meet this godly woman; He had chosen her to greatly influence my young spiritual life.

Venita actually did live by faith ("and not by hint," as she liked to say). She had a wonderful prayer life. When she heard the Holy Spirit tell her to do something or go somewhere, she went wherever God would lead her—Korea, Florida, or Blountville, Tennessee. The Holy Spirit led her to come to our area during the time when many of us had just been introduced to the baptism of the Holy Spirit and His spiritual gifts.

Venita's life was so full of love and the power of the Holy Spirit that she easily won my trust. I was still attending a denominational church at the time. But I was also leading Bible studies in our home, teaching hungry believers these fresh new truths of the Holy Spirit that we were learning. Though I was confident of Venita's genuine walk with God, she startled me by prophesying to me personally.

She declared that I was called to teach and preach and that I would travel around the world carrying the gospel. She was the first person to publicly confirm the calling of God on my life for ministry. After the Lord showed her His call on my life, she invited me to join her and minister in some revival meetings.

It was at her invitation that I first experienced teaching and preaching in a church setting. I remember how strange it felt to me to stand behind a pulpit and teach the Word of God. It seemed that just yesterday I was living my little ordinary life on Hermitage Drive, going to the office in the morning, grabbing fast food on the way home. My days had a sameness about them—boringly ordinary. Then suddenly (or so it seemed) I was standing behind pulpits and sharing my heart that was exploding with the wonderful truths I was learning from the Word of God.

It was hard for me to believe that a person's life could change this dramatically. Was this really me? I mean, had the real me been inside me all this time and I just hadn't met her yet? Venita told me that was exactly the case. She said I would be amazed at the things with which the Lord would entrust me. And she warned that I would need to accept the responsibility that goes with such a calling.

"What Do You Know About Fasting?"

One day, my mentor introduced me to a new facet of the Christian life. She asked me a simple question: "What do you know about fasting?" I answered weakly, "Well, I know Jesus talked about it. So I have been fasting for twenty-four hours each week. But what do I know about it? Really, nothing."

Venita began to share with me her experiences of fasting—fasts of short duration as well as longer ones. She told me how fasting had increased the level of anointing on her life so that she could pray for the sick and they would be healed. And, best of all, she said, "Fasting subdues the flesh in such a way that it increases one's sensitivity to hear from God."

Eager to hear from God, I embraced this truth of fasting. As I studied the Scriptures, the Holy Spirit confirmed to me that fasting must become a consistent part of our prayer lifestyle. I was so grateful that He had sent someone to begin to tell me how to order my life as a Christian. I felt so blessed that He would send me answers before I could even ask the questions. I wondered if Manoah felt like this when the angel came and told him and his wife how to raise their son Samson because of the call of God on his life (see Judg. 13:2-23).

The best thing about obvious supernatural intervention in your life is the mere fact of it; you were born for this—to discover your divine purpose. And every touch with divinity becomes a life-changing experience. It validates your personhood and satisfies the deepest longings of your soul for significance and purpose. Then you can say with the psalmist:

> As for me, I will behold thy face in righteousness: I shall be satisfied, when I awake, with thy likeness (Psalm 17:15).

> My soul shall be satisfied as with marrow and fatness; and my mouth shall praise thee with joyful lips: When I remember thee upon my bed, and meditate on thee in the night watches (Psalm 63:5-6).

BIBLICAL PURPOSE FOR FASTING

On one occasion, the disciples tried to deliver a boy who was tormented by a demon. His father brought him to the disciples and asked them to use their authority to cast it out. They could not. When Jesus arrived on the scene, He cast it out and healed the boy, returning him to his father.

Then the disciples asked the same question that many believers ask when they do not get answers to their prayers:

> And Jesus said unto them, Because of your unbelief: for verily I say unto you, If ye have faith as a grain of mustard seed, ye shall say unto this mountain, Remove hence to yonder place; and it shall remove; and nothing shall be

impossible unto you. Howbeit this kind goeth not out but by prayer and fasting (Matthew 17:20-21).

As usual, Jesus spoke directly to their question, telling them the truth about their dilemma and giving them the answer to it. *Unbelief* was the problem; prayer and fasting was the solution. It is not the answer many of us like to hear.

According to Jesus' answer, fasting and prayer can increase the faith in our hearts and help us to overcome unbelief. Unbelief due to a lack of prayer and fasting kept the disciples from the place of authority required for deliverance and victory over the devil.

Even in the Old Testament, fasting had a divine purpose. In the book of Jonah, the king of Ninevah called a fast when he heard the judgment of God against them. Even the cattle had to fast. And God relented from the punishment He had threatened against their city (see Jonah 3).

Isaiah declared that the true fast was to set the oppressed free, to break yokes of bondage and lift unbearable burdens, to feed the hungry and help the poor. When fulfilled, the promises to that people were impressive: Your light will break forth, your health shall spring forth speedily, and the glory of the Lord shall be your reward (see Isa. 58:6-8).

Daniel fasted in order to receive revelation from God regarding His covenant promises to Israel. Though he had to fast and pray twenty-one days, his fasting and prayer released angels to overcome the evil Prince of Persia resisting God's people in the realm of the Spirit. And Daniel received the divine revelation he sought (see Dan. 10:11-14).

In the New Testament, the apostle Paul declared that he was in "fastings" often (see 2 Cor. 11:26). And he said that he continually kept his body under control, to "bring it into subjection: lest that by any means, when I have preached to others, I myself should be a castaway" (1 Cor. 9:27).

Anyone who has fasted understands the power of a fast to break addictions and to subdue the desires of the flesh to the authority of the

Spirit of God. There are victories in life that must be sought through prayer and fasting; prayer alone, no matter how fervent, is not enough.

"When You Fast..."

Jesus did not consider fasting an option for those who wanted to be more spiritual. He presented it as a command to be obeyed. He did not say to His disciples, "If you fast...," but "When you fast..." (see Matt. 6:16). Then He gave them specific instructions for doing so. It is a great day on your spiritual journey when you discover the blessing of fasting.

Without fasting as an integral part of our church's prayer lifestyle, I do not believe we would have seen the miracles and breakthroughs we have experienced through the years. During those early years of establishing our church, I fasted so much that I sometimes couldn't remember if I was fasting or not. When someone would offer me something to eat, I would have to ask myself, "Am I fasting today?"

I only mention this to make the point that the Holy Spirit taught me to fast often. The weekly twenty-four hour fast that I had adopted early in my Christian walk was a given. After that, there have been fasts of varying length and intensity throughout my life. If I neglected fasting, the Holy Spirit was always faithful to convict me and get me back on the path.

For many years, we have fasted and prayed together as a congregation the first full week in January. During that week, we meet daily to pray together. We direct our prayers systematically, seeking direction for every area of the church during the year ahead. After that, we encourage weekly fasting throughout the year on an individual basis.

Fasting is not about being hungry or doing without. Fasting is about quieting the drives of the soul and body and drawing near to God. It is about obedience to the commands of Jesus and receiving the rewards He promises. And it is about breaking bondages that keep us bound to the will of our flesh, the will of people, and the will of the devil.

The empowering that comes through fasting and prayer would prepare me for the challenges that lay ahead. When I received the baptism of the Holy Spirit, I was not aware of the magnitude of the challenges that I would face in the days ahead, but God was, and He was equipping me.

I was still basking in the first love of salvation and marveling at the divine change in direction for our lives. I would soon discover that these wonderful spiritual experiences were not just to make me "feel good"; they were necessary empowerment for the task God was about to reveal to us.

So there are revivals to come; there are wonderful things to be done, when we can be lost in the Spirit until the Spirit prays through to victory.

—Smith Wigglesworth[1]

CHAPTER 5

REVIVAL FIRES

FROM THE DAY MY HUSBAND and I received Jesus as our Savior at that Methodist Youth Retreat, life has never been the same for us on any level. After our initiation into ministry in Methodist churches with our youth group, I was invited to give my testimony in churches and in Methodist Lay Witness Missions. I would share what I had just learned from my study of the Scriptures, and God did the rest. People were saved, and others were inspired to commit their lives more fully to God.

Then, not long after I received the baptism of the Holy Spirit, a pastor asked me to preach a revival in a community eighty miles away from where we lived. I had never attempted such a thing, but I didn't tell him that. Every evening I drove the eighty miles to this small church, preached and led the revival service, and then drove eighty miles home—for ten days.

During the daytime, I asked some praying women to join me in prayer for the services. During the nights, the Holy Spirit moved powerfully during the service, causing men, women, boys, and girls to surrender their lives to God. There were fantastic spiritual break-throughs in many lives. Men who were known in the community as alcoholics and others known as "sinners" wept their way to salvation.

For ten days we prayed, and for ten nights I ministered to that church and community.

What is so wonderful about a real revival, led and empowered by the Holy Spirit, is the element of surprise. No two services were alike. Night after night during the services, people spontaneously stood to repent and ask the church's forgiveness for offenses and other wrongdoing.

People would seek me out privately to ask for prayer to be delivered from deep-rooted, often shameful habits. The Holy Spirit had convicted them to get their lives in order. The church leaders told me that, to their knowledge, everyone who came to those meetings unsaved received Jesus as their Savior. A few of the people who received Jesus during those meetings have relocated and are in our church today.

The Fire Was Spreading.

The entire community seemed to be talking about revival. Other pastors asked me to speak in their churches, and school principals asked me to speak to their students. I was learning that when a revival spirit invades an area, people do bold and unusual things.

I was visiting in a home at the invitation of the local college president. The pastor of an influential church in the area was there with one of his members, a wealthy man who was also an alcoholic. During our conversation, this man startled me when he suddenly turned to his pastor and said, "Pastor, this lady needs to preach at our church Sunday, and you need a break."

The pastor just quietly responded, "Whatever you think."

The following Sunday, I preached in that affluent church a message entitled "The Rich Fool." My text was from the parable of Jesus about the man whose security rested in his personal wealth:

The ground of a certain rich man brought forth plentifully: And he thought within himself, saying, What shall I do, because I have no room where to bestow my fruits? And he said, This will I do: I will pull down my barns, and build greater…And I will say to my soul, Soul…take thine ease, eat, drink, and be merry (Luke 12:16-19).

But Jesus called him a fool and said that he would die that night because he had laid up treasure for himself and was not rich toward God (see Luke 12:20-21). He said this was a picture of everyone whose treasure is earthly and who does not treasure relationship with God.

As I shared this truth of Jesus' parable, I glimpsed the displeasure on the face of one older lady, who was wearing a fur and elegant jewelry. She turned her face away, looking glumly at the stained glass window at the end of the pew where she always sat. But the wealthy alcoholic was also listening, and he seemed very happy to hear the truth.

I was learning to simply trust in that daily prayer with my little band of believing women. We continually petitioned God to continue His mighty works of salvation and deliverance. Watching God work among people of my heritage in these mountains, I understood that believing prayer swallows up all fears and doubts.

Who was I to reap such a harvest? I was just a little woman who was willing to say *yes* to every open door of opportunity to share Jesus in this community. I was learning that fervent prayer has the power to change the spiritual atmosphere in a home, a church, and an entire community. In ways that are still mysterious to me, I saw that earnest petitions for the souls of people released them from their darkened minds into a realm of hope.

PIERCING THE DARKNESS WITH HIS LIGHT

By the time the next revival started in Paint Lick, a nearby mountain community, I was gaining confidence. If I would keep my team praying, God would keep working His wonders. However, that confidence was soon to be challenged by powerful forces of spiritual darkness working in this community.

It was Halloween. There was a kind of dense darkness that we could feel all around us as we drove through the mountain hollow. I have to admit that I felt a little apprehensive. Some things you just do, even if you have to do it afraid. Maybe that is what the psalmist meant when he declared, "What time I am afraid, I will trust in thee" (Ps. 56:3). But oh, the rewards of obedience!

Twelve people attended the first service. It was not a wonderful start to revival, as we had experienced it in other places. But as I preached the wonderful love of Jesus that had become a reality to me, people responded. Attendance grew so much that the church was full, and people had to sit on the floor. Once again, souls were being rescued from spiritual darkness to the redeeming light of His love.

After ten days, the pastor begged me to stay and continue the meetings. I didn't know much about how long to extend a series of meetings, but I remembered one of my early mentors had told me, "Always stop the meetings when you're going up. Don't wait until interest and attendance begin to wane." We were definitely still going up, so I ended the meetings, confident that God would finish the work He had begun in that community.

CRASH COURSE IN EVANGELISM

In this "crash course" of evangelism, I learned the secret to the powerful results of that revival—*praying in the Spirit*. I'm not talking about just a quick-breathed request for His help, but about waiting on God in prayer. I am talking about asking for His power to be manifest in changing lives, seeking His wisdom and yielding to His empowering for the message that would touch hearts. Allowing the Holy Spirit to fill our hearts with compassion for hurting, lost people who need a Savior released His power for salvation.

I noted that in Jesus' ministry He did His miracles during the day, and He prayed at night. The Scriptures record some occasions when Jesus prayed all night. It was His lifestyle of relationship with His Father.

Since our meetings were at night, we had to pray during the day. Yet, the pattern was the same for us as I saw in Jesus' life: intense prayer specifically to bring the Father's redeeming power into needy lives. Jesus said He could do only what He saw the Father doing (see John 5:30,36). We began to understand clearly the reality of Jesus' words to His followers: "...Without Me ye can do nothing" (John 15:5).

ANN'S HEALING

After I received the baptism of the Holy Spirit, I learned to pray for others so that they could receive this empowerment of the Holy Spirit as well. Doors were still opening for ministry to Methodist churches, which I happily accepted. One evening after I had spoken on the empowering of the Holy Spirit, a beautiful lady named Ann asked if I would pray for her to receive the baptism of the Holy Spirit.

Not only did she receive the answer to her request, but she was also instantly healed of tumors that were lodged throughout her body. The Scriptures teach that the Lord "is able to do exceeding abundantly above all that we ask or think, according to the power that worketh in us" (Eph. 3:20).

I didn't know anything about Ann's need for healing, so I wasn't able to "ask or think" that she might be healed in that same moment. God simply gave to her more than she expected. With that wonderful touch from God, Ann was hooked for life. Now, as a precious octogenarian, Ann continues to serve God faithfully. She is a personal intercessor for me, and she champions Jesus' desire to make all His children completely whole.

During that season, I continually studied the Scriptures, seeking to become more acquainted with the Holy Spirit's role in helping us pray:

> *And the Holy Spirit helps us in our distress. For we don't even know what we should pray for, nor how we should pray. But the Holy Spirit prays for us with groanings that cannot be expressed in words. And the Father who knows*

all hearts knows what the Spirit is saying, for the Spirit pleads for us believers in harmony with God's own will (Romans 8:26-27 NLT).

As I gave myself to praying in the Spirit and waiting on the Lord, I was learning to hear His voice more clearly. By now I had advanced beyond my "Look in tender mercy" prayers and had learned that God would answer many kinds of prayers. I also understood that developing a strong prayer life was absolutely necessary for all believers who want to do the will of God.

Little by little, the Holy Spirit began to show me that the calling of God on my life was to do a specific work that would bring God glory. It was the greatest challenge I had faced yet in my journey into God. Gaining this understanding of my destiny pressed me into new dependency on God, which led me into new dimensions of prayer.

What I felt God was asking me to do was absolutely impossible through my own natural abilities. I would soon learn that it was also beyond our financial means as a couple or even a small Bible study group. In God's divine wisdom, He hid from us some of these details of the path of destiny that lay ahead.

*God's cause is committed to men; God com-
mits Himself to men. Praying men are the
vice-regents of God; they do His work and
carry out His plans.*

—E.M. Bounds[1]

CHAPTER 6

"I WANT YOU TO BUILD A PLACE"

DURING THOSE FIRST FEW YEARS after I was saved, I enrolled in a local Bible college to study the Scriptures formally. I continued leading our home prayer group and Bible study, and I preached wherever I was invited. My husband, John, had completed his college degree and was working as a research chemist for a large manufacturer in the area.

I enjoyed leading the Bible study in our home, teaching people who were hungry to know God and to study His Word. The Sermon on the Mount was fascinating to me. I began to understand that it revealed a comprehensive lifestyle of godly attitudes and actions for all believers.

In my religious training, the projection had been that the Sermon on the Mount was simply an unreachable ideal. While it might represent "gold standard" for the conduct of Christians, it was presumed that no one could make it an actual way of life. It was generally understood that only Jesus could live a lifestyle like He described.

Now, reading the Word with new eyes and filled with child-like faith, I decided to believe Jesus' message exactly the way He said it: Turn the other cheek, walk the second mile, don't allow lust in your thoughts (see Matt. 6). Embracing these biblical principles for living the Christian life was a major shift from the religious paradigm that most of us had known.

IT SEEMED RADICAL

Change always comes hard. Radical change takes your breath away and ignites all your natural defenses. Attempting to adopt a religious paradigm that embraced the Sermon on the Mount as an everyday lifestyle—well, that was radical.

Why would Jesus' commandments appear radical to born-again Christians? It must be because the American Church has settled for less than what Jesus taught. Someone has said that when *subnormal* becomes *normal*, normal becomes *abnormal!*

To actually attempt to live the principles of the Sermon on the Mount, for some, seems abnormal. In our minds, we were simply shifting our religious paradigm from subnormal to normal, choosing to live the principles that Jesus taught.

As we continued to pray together in our Bible study group, the Holy Spirit began to indicate that some of us should join together to build a ministry where we could live these commandments of Jesus—a place where people could come to receive these truths of God and see them reflected in our lives.

We began to sense that the Lord was challenging us to renounce the "status quo." He wanted us to discover what He would do if we allowed Him to work these "love principles" into our daily lifestyles. During a time of intense prayer about our future, the Holy Spirit spoke to me like this:

> I want you to build a place where the commandments of Jesus will become a reality in everyday life. I want it to be a place where people can give their all to Me and minister to the needs of people.

These instructions were so supernatural that they seemed natural, in a sense. Here was the answer to our desire to live the Sermon on the Mount and share our love for Jesus with others. Yet, was it possible that God would ask such a thing of our little group? *How would they respond?* I wondered.

ORDINARY PEOPLE; EXTRAORDINARY VISION

When I shared with our home group the latest instructions the Holy Spirit had given me, there were six families who caught the vision with John and me. They were willing to take a risk to fulfill the desire of their hearts to demonstrate the love of Jesus to the world. Together, we made the decision to begin to look for the "place" the Holy Spirit had indicated. It seemed that was the next step for us to fulfill this vision God had given us.

Experiencing the glorious thrill and the gravity of that decision, I felt I could relate to Mother Teresa's desire to do "something beautiful for God." That is what I longed to do—something that would please God's heart. I did not know in that moment what would be the results of our obedience to the Holy Spirit's command. Eventually, it would bring His presence among us in such power that He would enable us to impact other ministries, churches, and even nations.

We were all very ordinary people, but we were filled with an extraordinary zeal to fulfill the vision God had given us. Later, we found in the Scriptures that our ordinariness actually "qualified" us to do the work God called us to do:

For ye see your calling, brethren, how that not many wise men after the flesh, not many mighty, not many noble, are called (I Corinthians 1:26).

Jesus chose fishermen to be His disciples and even a loathed tax collector, Matthew. His list of followers included Mary Magdalene, out of whom He cast seven devils, and Chuza, a steward's wife, Joanna, and other women (see Luke 8). All were ordinary people who dared to become a part of an extraordinary vision.

Our list of six families included Ann, the lady who was healed of tumors, and her husband, Lowell, the building contractor. There were our friends, Judy, a former beauty queen, and her husband, Tommy, a high school football star.

Another couple, J.R. and Linda, who clawed their way out of an ordinary life, readily embraced the vision. Don and Shirley, who were saved in the first revival I ever preached, joined with us. Harold and Barbara Barnes, friends who were hungry for God, had joined our Bible study and were eager to help. And a special lady, my sister, Glenna, who was a single mom, also wanted to help.

With John and me, we were seven families (some with children) that were about to attempt a work for God that none of us had ever imagined. It is no wonder that we threw ourselves into prayer, dependent on the mercy of God to help us make sense of our seemingly "radical" future.

Faith for "The Place"

I began searching for the "place" where we could do what God was calling us to do. As our small group continued to pray together, the Holy Spirit led me to the exact property where we would establish the work to which He had called us.

I found an advertisement in the local newspaper that said, "Indian Springs Area, 160 acres more or less." When I read that, the Holy Spirit spoke to my heart, "This is your land." So, I invited my friend, Judy, to go with me to look at this property. We drove onto the 160-acre farmland property that boasted an old, tin-roofed farmhouse and a run-down barn.

As we did, the Holy Spirit spoke again to me an unusual phrase that I would fully understand as the ministry developed. I did not know how expansive the ministry would be, nor did I understand that this day was the first step to developing a ministry that would impact the nations. I did not really know yet what the ministry was to be. The Holy Spirit's words to me were all I needed at the time. He said, "What it is, this is where it is"—meaning, "Regarding what I have called you to do, this is where it is to be done."

I did not have a blueprint for what God was asking us to build. In that moment, there was just the land, Jesus, and me. Of course, I had the Lord's promise that the Holy Spirit would lead us into all truth.

And I was filled with a deep desire to please God. I was completely dependent on His leadership and step-by-step revelation to do what He asked.

When I took my husband to look at the property, he was, well, less than enthused. It was dawning on his scientific, calculating mind that this thing was really going to happen. The dream of a "place" that was birthed in my heart was going to dramatically impact his future as well as mine—and ours. He had no intention at that time of selling our home to move to a place that I thought would fulfill my partially understood mandate from God. That would take a work of the Holy Spirit in his heart.

God Got His Man into the Land

As I continued to minister to our home group, God laid on my heart a sermon called, "Abraham, God's Man in the Land." The Holy Spirit had revealed to me that in order to do His will in the earth, establish His people, and set them free, He always needed to have "a man in the land" who would do His bidding. Of course, that could apply to each of us who would choose to be a vessel for God's work in the earth.

Afterward, I decided to meet just with the six families who seemed to share my vision for "a place." We prayed earnestly together for the will of God and for courage to be obedient. We prayed together about purchasing property to begin the fulfillment of the vision.

As we prayed and wept together that day, surrendering our lives to God, John prayed aloud, honestly questioning God's purpose for our future. He poured out his heart about his struggle with such a change in lifestyle and an uncertain future. Then, in the next moment, I was astonished to hear his prayer and his tone change directions—180 degrees.

I listened as my husband blurted out, with great resolve, "Lord, I'm your man. I'll be your man in the land!" Later, he expressed his own amazement at the words he heard coming out of his mouth with such zeal. In that moment, God had done a transforming work in his heart. He was willing and eager to pursue this divine adventure that would change his life forever.

From that day, John had no further questions. He became "God's man in the land" who directed the physical and financial ministry from day one. God has given him great wisdom and a counseling gift to help other people and church leaders in the areas of finance and property management.

If John had known from the beginning that "our" calling was actually going to involve his oversight of never-ending property development, building, and management during the next forty years, I can only imagine what his response might have been in that moment. I now understand that "It is the glory of God to conceal a thing..." (Prov. 25:2). As the vision has unfolded through the years, John's heart of compassion has been enlarged to desire to fulfill all God had called us to do.

LEARNING TO PRAY THE SCRIPTURES

As I was praying about the property I felt we should buy, the Holy Spirit began to impress upon me a biblical principle to be used in claiming and acquiring territory. I read the passage where the Lord was instructing Joshua about entering the Promised Land. He spoke these words to him:

> *Moses my servant is dead; now therefore arise, go over this Jordan, thou, and all this people, unto the land which I do give to them, even to the children of Israel. Every place that the sole of your foot shall tread upon, that have I given unto you, as I said unto Moses* (Joshua 1:2-3).

I was impressed that God wanted me to do as Joshua was instructed to do: "Every place that the sole of your foot shall tread upon, that have I given unto you" (Josh. 1:3). So, I walked the entire perimeter of the farmland where I felt God had led me. As I did, I claimed this property for the work of God to which He had called us. All of this was new to me, but it wouldn't be long before I discovered that it worked.

There was a man in our church who was a bank president. Try as he would, he was not able to persuade the owner of the property to cooperate with us on a workable plan to purchase his property. Then one day, the owner of the property came to me. He said that his wife was a Presbyterian, dedicated to the doctrine of the sovereignty of God. He looked at me sheepishly and told me she had spoken some convincing words to him about our desire to purchase his property.

He said, "My wife told me, 'Vernon, I believe that woman [speaking of me] is a woman of God. And if she is, and if He has called her to do a work for Him on your land, there's nothing you can do about it.'"

It was just what I needed; if his wife had been an angel, she couldn't have done a better job of fighting for my cause. At the moment, we wanted to buy 100 acres of his 160-acre farm. He did not want to sell us any of the property if we were not going to buy all of it.

You can imagine how surprised I was that day when he said to me, "Here, take a pencil and draw a line to divide the property. Choose what you want."

I wondered if this was what Lot felt like when Abraham told him:

This arguing between our herdsmen has got to stop. . . .I'll tell you what we'll do. Take your choice of any section of the land you want, and we will separate. If you want that area over there, then I'll stay here. If you want to stay in this area, then I'll move on to another place (see Genesis 13:8-9).

I had obeyed God's word to do as Joshua had done and walk the land that God wanted to give us. So I knew the layout of the land well enough to do just what the owner asked and choose what we wanted. I marked the map accordingly, establishing the boundaries for "the place" God had designated that we build.

Through that situation, I learned that sometimes the Holy Spirit will increase our faith greatly by giving us specific instructions to follow, exactly as He did in Scripture. He can also help us pray prophetic prayers for our situation that come right from the Scriptures. When that happens, we can pray and act with confidence and faith that we will have what we asked.

God's favor goes before us when we break through in prayer to conquer the hindering power of the enemy in the Spirit realm. Through prevailing prayer, He will use other people and even angels to give us success in doing His will.

The man who mobilizes the Christian church
to pray will make the greatest contribution
to world evangelization in history.

—Andrew Murray[1]

CHAPTER 7

OUR COMMITMENT IS TESTED

As a result of negotiating the purchase of 100 acres of this farm, we needed $40,000 for a down payment on the property. It was a daunting amount based on 1973 wages and economy. I shared with these families that John and I were planning to sell our home and put the equity we received toward the down payment. I simply encouraged them to do what they felt the Holy Spirit wanted them to do to help make the vision a reality.

I was careful to make sure these families did only what they felt the Holy Spirit was telling them to do to help raise these funds. We formed a non-profit corporation to which donations could be made individually. Everyone gave sacrificially.

For some, it was the equity from the sale of their homes. For others, it was the proceeds from the sale of a boat or other valuable possessions. I was humbled to see how God had worked in each of their hearts, filling them with joy to be a part of this vision God had given us.

I remembered Jesus' words: "Where your treasure is, there will your heart be also" (Luke 12:34). In those acts of sacrificial giving, we were made aware that God had truly transferred our affections from our own personal gain to the heavenly vision. We were giving our "treasure" to help establish the kingdom of God.

After raising the down payment, we had to secure the remaining purchase of 100 acres of this beautiful land with its rolling hills. John and I and these six families signed a promissory note for $177,000 (equivalent to about $335,000 today) to that end. Taking this step of faith almost took our breath away. We were not only committing our finances to God, but we were committing our lives to one another to do the work of God for which we did not yet have a blueprint.

During the next three years, the miracles of divine provision, the exciting unfolding of the vision, and the dozens of changed lives we witnessed confirmed to us that God had been leading us supernaturally into our divine destiny. That gave us the faith to sign another note for $250,000 to purchase the remaining 60 acres of this beautiful farm.

We could not have imagined then that God would also provide for a beautifully developed campus, spacious sanctuary, and other educational and conference center facilities, including a lovely guesthouse. Nor could we have imagined how the property would have increased in value during these four decades. It was with great joy that we burned the notes in 1988, only fifteen years later; because of God's supernatural provision, we were debt free much sooner than we expected to be.

Yet for us the greatest joy is that this is still "the place" where we are living to obey the commandments of Jesus, to help hurting people, and to become a house of prayer for all nations.

In one of our prayer meetings, Judy felt impressed that the name of this place should be *Shekinah,* which in Hebrew means "the glory of God" or "the manifest presence of God"; it refers to the presence of God that dwelt in Moses' tabernacle. That was our desire above all else, to establish a place where the manifest presence of God would dwell. So, we named our place Shekinah Church.

ARE YOU SURE?

In the minds of family and friends, it took a little while to resolve questions regarding our vision. To the frugal, hardworking people in our area, sacrificing our personal security for a plan to pour our lives into such an undertaking seemed highly unusual. Some cheered our zeal to do a "good" thing and to make a difference. Some doubted: "Why are you going *way out there?*"

To be sure, rolling hills, country roads, and beautiful farmland was all that surrounded our property in 1973. We did not know that Interstate Highway 81, under construction at the time, would pass within 1.5 miles of our church property. And we did not know how important it would be that we were conveniently located near the Tri-Cities Airport, only 7 minutes away.

As Shekinah Church grew into a thriving local congregation as well as a conference center, hosting regional and national training conferences, thousands of people would be grateful that it was located so near to the airport. Twenty years later, a newspaper article referred to our exit off Highway 81 as "the downtown of the Tri-Cities area." It is filled with hotels, restaurants, and other businesses. Luxurious subdivisions surround us on what was once adjacent farmland.

A local banker credited the development of our property as the impetus for much of the development and growth of the area. We could not take credit for "choosing" a perfect location for the "place." We knew that it was through prayer that the Holy Spirit showed us where it should be. But, in short, we are no longer "way out there."

MAKING "NEWS"

Once word spread about of our ambitious endeavor to establish a place where we could live the commandments of Jesus and help hurting people, the area newspaper came to get the "story." They thought it was remarkable that people would sacrifice their own lifestyle and personal security to commit themselves to work for God on such a scale.

Reporters came to the property and took pictures of John and me in front of the dilapidated barn that graced our "farm" and in which we held our first services. We were amazed when our story filled half of the front page of the Sunday edition, under the headline, "Living What They Preach."

MORE MIRACLES

Because we were learning to cover every situation with prayer, the Holy Spirit continually led us through a series of miracles until the place we envisioned began to be a reality before our eyes. Neither John nor I were professional developers, builders, or financiers. The operative word for what we have accomplished since the day we were born again is *dependence.* We were totally dependent upon God; that is why we learned to pray.

In the same chapter where we read that God didn't call "many wise," the Scripture also declares that Christ Jesus "...became to us *wisdom* from God, and righteousness and sanctification, and redemption" (I Cor. 1:30 NASB, emphasis mine). We understood our need for His wisdom and for the Holy Spirit to lead us into all truth as Jesus promised (see John 16:13).

The Holy Spirit knows everything about everything; He is God, the Third Person of the Trinity. He was there in creation, "hovering over the face of the waters" (Gen. 1:2 NKJV). When God spoke the Word: "Let there be...," the Holy Spirit performed it. The Holy Spirit, in response to our obedience, would fulfill the word that God had spoken to us to build a place for His glory. To say that we have experienced some dramatic moments along the way would be an understatement.

"LADY, THIS SIMPLY CAN'T BE DONE"

Our first development project was the construction of a road into the property. Again, we sought the guidance of the Holy Spirit in prayer. We did not presume to know how to develop such a large tract of land, especially since we did not know the entirety of the "divine plan" we were following so boldly.

We hired a man with a bulldozer who was accustomed to grading out roads in the mountains. We asked him to lay out the path for our road. When he arrived, he looked it over and then threw up his hands in consternation. "Oh, lady, we will hit so much rock through there; it simply can't be done. I don't even want to touch this job. We'll have to blast and dig to get you a road."

At this point, he began to just shake his head and step backward, as if he wanted to get away from me. I threw up an S.O.S. to the Holy Spirit. Then I gave him a proposition.

"How about this?" I offered. "I'll pay you fifty dollars an hour if you will simply follow me with your dozer as I lead you through the woods from here to the clearing." He looked at me in disbelief, saw my determination, mumbled something, and then—agreed.

I don't know if I felt more relief or dismay. What I didn't say was that, in that moment, the Holy Spirit had spoken to me that as God led Moses through the wilderness, He was well able to lead me along this rocky ridge and through this little wooded area to make a road for His place.

That was the most prayerful journey I had ever taken to that moment. My continued prayer was not profound or complicated. I just said something like, "OK, Jesus, if you don't guide my steps, I'm a goner. Please help my unbelief. You can do anything!"

I began to lead that man on his bulldozer through the woods, around protruding rocks and ancient trees, breathing out my simple prayer with every step. As I followed the contour of the ridge walking in front of that dozer, there were a few large overhanging outcroppings of rock, but they always ended up well to the side of the proposed roadbed. After twisting and turning for three quarters of a mile, we finally came into the clearing. We had a road, and I felt like I could breathe again.

That dozer operator couldn't believe it. He just shook his head and said he couldn't figure out what happened to all the rock he knew had to be along that ridge. He received his wages, and we asked God to bless him. We knew we had received another miracle.

How do you receive miracles like this? We were learning to yield to the Holy Spirit and receive His divine guidance. The idea of walking in front of the bulldozer might be considered "a word of wisdom or knowledge," which the Scriptures teach are gifts of the Holy Spirit (see I Cor. 12:8). The courage to do so could have been a "gift of faith" as well. The Holy Spirit places His thoughts, His divine wisdom, and His courage into our hearts when we sincerely seek to do His will.

When we learn to ask the Lord to release the gifts of the Holy Spirit, He begins to give them to believers for the fulfillment of His purposes. When we keep our hearts open to Him by seeking Him daily, early in the day, we make room for the Holy Spirit to show us how to pray and how to walk throughout the day. That is what miracles are made of.

We are supposed to be so dependent on the Holy Spirit that we hear Him speak to us and guide us in every situation. Jesus taught that some believers would face persecution and be taken to court for their faith. Even in that hour, He told them that the Holy Spirit would tell them what to say:

> *But when they deliver you up, take no thought how or what ye shall speak: for it shall be given you in that same hour what ye shall speak. For it is not ye that speak, but the Spirit of your Father which speaketh in you* (Matthew 10:19-20).

LEARNING TO PRAY FOR FINANCIAL MIRACLES

At the time we purchased our property, it was clear that six families did not need 100 acres of farmland. Nor were we able to make payments on that kind of mortgage without supernatural intervention. And, as I said, there was no blueprint for the place God wanted us to build for His glory. He was leading us one step at a time into a ministry that would ultimately touch the nations.

When we began to plan how to develop the property we had bought, we realized that we would need for God to miraculously intervene again to meet our financial needs. First, we needed a loan to begin building our facilities. I made an appointment to talk to a bank president about our exciting life-vision—to have a place where the commandments of Jesus could be lived and to help others realize their destinies. In that moment, that was all we knew about God's plan for His place, Sheki-nah Church.

The bank president listened very respectfully to my story. When I finished, I explained the financial help we felt we needed to begin building. I waited quietly for his response, holding my breath for what seemed an eternity. Thoughtfully, he slowly adjusted himself in his high-backed, leather swivel chair so that he could look directly into my eyes.

"Mrs. Curran, I think this is one of the most noble causes I have ever heard."

Yes, yes, go on, I said inside my head, still holding my breath. I must have reflected my inward hope in my face.

"But we can't commit our bank to something this unusual. We really want no part of it."

Involuntarily, I let out my breath and traded it for another deep one. Disappointment flooded my heart. Awkwardly, I turned to go.

"It was kind of you to listen," I almost whispered.

Leaving that bank, I turned right and walked to another bank three blocks away. The Lord had taught me what to do when He showed me what He wanted me to do and people said "no." I am to translate that "no" into "Find another way."

At the second bank, I spoke with a vice president. He was younger and seemed more favorably impressed than the first banker. And, after all, I had already practiced my speech; it wasn't as hard to articulate this time.

Still, after my first bank encounter, I could scarcely believe this banker's response. He simply said, "The board is meeting this afternoon. I will take your request to them. But you need to know, it's a long shot."

I replied matter-of-factly, "While you're in the board meeting, I will call a prayer meeting. We will see what God will do."

Later that day, he called me and said, almost sheepishly, "Your folks must know how to pray. The board said 'Yes.'" Then he volunteered, "You know the chairman of the board is a Presbyterian, and he startled us when he said, 'This may really be a work of God, and maybe we are to be the lending institution for them. If that is true, we don't want to miss out on it.'"

In a businesslike manner, that I hoped covered my surprise and delight, I thanked him. We made an appointment to finalize arrangements with them. Then I hung up the phone and began dancing around my living room, clapping my hands and praising God for such a miracle.

Are you beginning to understand why I had no choice but to learn to pray? To obey God with this level of commitment, I couldn't risk being the victim of ill-founded plans or people's opinions. The greatest hazard we faced was to fail to hear the voice of God in prayer and not get the answers we needed to move forward with His plan.

We were completely dependent on God to show us what He wanted us to do as well as how to do it. We were committing our lives to bring glory to His name. Failure would bring reproach, not just to us, but to His wonderful name.

I learned to pray. Our fledgling congregation learned to pray. And God has been faithful to reward our petitions as He has promised us in His Word that He would do. Everything we have accomplished has been preceded by and bathed in prayer. The Holy Spirit has always been faithful to lead us into new dimensions of prayer.

The prayer power has never been tried to its full capacity. If we want to see mighty wonders of divine power and grace wrought in the place of weakness, failure and disappointment, let us answer God's standing challenge, "Call unto me, and I will answer thee, and show thee great and mighty things which thou knowest not!"

—*J. Hudson Taylor*[1]

CHAPTER 8

THE VISION IS GROWING

OUR FIRST SANCTUARY WAS THE large old barn located on the property we had purchased. It was complete with a "cathedral ceiling" and was even air conditioned—naturally—through the openings in the sides designed to aerate the hay. We enjoyed wonderful services and prayer times during the months we met in that barn loft.

How many twentieth-century preachers do you know who have tried out their sermons on chickens sitting quietly on the stair rail of a barn, occasionally clucking their approval? The fragrance of hay and the unannounced visit of the occasional field mouse were constant reminders that our sanctuary was a humble place. One could not help recalling a lowly manger in a Bethlehem stable.

Thoughts of those precious encounters with the Holy Spirit during the early beginnings of this ministry fill us with certain nostalgia for those days of "small beginnings." It was from this humble beginning that the Holy Spirit confirmed our calling to fulfill a unique, worldwide mission. He sent to us outstanding preachers and prophets who, without knowing, consistently confirmed the heavenly vision for our lives.

For example, we were amazed when South African Evangelist Robert Thom showed up to preach in our barn sanctuary. Born in Cape Town, he was known internationally as one of the most powerful healing evangelists of the twentieth century, "who moved in the prophetic realm and witnessed signs, wonders and miracles in his life and ministry. Walking in a powerful anointing, having an intimate relationship with God and unquestionable faith and trust in God, he saw many powerful miracles take place in his daily life"[2] A coworker of an early Pentecostal Apostle of Faith, F.F. Bosworth, Robert Thom traveled throughout South Africa, witnessing and experiencing the miraculous power of God.

As if it were yesterday, I can hear Robert Thom's booming voice, with his impressive South African accent, prophesying to me in that barn:

> You are thinking of other nations, and you know God's
> work has got to be done there. But you feel like your feet
> are in cement. I tell you tonight you are ready to travel. The
> nations are calling you. I am sending you first to this nation.
> You will travel from border to border of your country. And
> in other nations, I am calling you to a dark-skinned people
> who will find a large place in your heart.

His words shook me to the core of my being. Thinking about other nations? Perhaps. But not now. At present I was engaging all my faculties for the challenging work that was right here. Yet as I was to learn, Robert Thom had prophesied my destiny before I had even allowed myself to dwell on such a daunting challenge as ministering in the nations.

I wondered if this was how Abraham felt when God told him to "look to the stars of the heavens" to imagine the number of his progeny when as yet he did not have a son (see Gen. 22:17; 26:4). How finite and insignificant we can feel when we receive a word from the Spirit of God projecting a future that we have not imagined. It would be only a few years before this prophetic word would be fulfilled, regarding both my travel in the United States and to other nations.

MORE CHALLENGES

In the summer months, we were thankful for the lovely, natural air-conditioning in our barn. However, when October came, we had to face the fact that our air-conditioned barn loft was not *heated*. With winter approaching, we were once again facing our need of another miracle to meet the challenges of the unfolding of the vision God had given us.

I prayed and asked the Holy Spirit to show me what to do. Once again, He responded clearly, "You can build a simple building that will seat a hundred people. There are some people in your congregation who will each give one thousand dollars if you simply announce the need."

As usual, I was a little unprepared to hear such specific instructions from God. But I have learned that when the Holy Spirit speaks, He leaves no guesswork. His voice is neither unclear nor confusing. Yet, I must confess, it is sometimes a challenge to my faith to receive His word.

It didn't seem to me that we had many people who would immediately give that amount of money. They were already giving their best to pay the mortgage and other expenses of the ministry. But when I announced the need, the response was immediate. Designing a small addition to the original farmhouse to seat one hundred people, we built our first real sanctuary for $10,000 cash.

I wonder if we truly appreciate God giving us the Holy Spirit to teach us all things and guide us into all truth (see John 16:13). I sometimes hear Christians say the Holy Spirit spoke to them in prayer. Yet they still seem perplexed and cannot understand what they are to do. That has not been my experience when the Holy Spirit speaks to me.

He is the Spirit of truth, and He is well able to speak with great clarity. He knows the future of God's purposes to be fulfilled in your life. When you understand who He is, you have taken a giant step toward praying in faith. And you will receive divine direction with confidence to do His will.

GROWING PAINS

In less than three years, we had outgrown our little sanctuary. We continued to pray daily for divine direction and supernatural provision as we had done from the beginning. God was faithfully providing the funds for our loan payments through tithes and offerings.

During those first seven years of the ministry, my husband continued to work as a research chemist. I had resigned my secretarial position, choosing to live on John's income as we poured our time and energies, as well as our financial means, into this unfolding vision. We learned that you can never out-give God. As someone has said, "His shovel is always bigger than yours."

I prayed with a small group each day, and as the vision presented greater challenges, these faithful people helped me to earnestly petition God for His purposes to be fulfilled in our lives. Our little group of prayer partners began to ask that God would show us clearly what to do about our need for a larger sanctuary.

I am aware that the "normal" thing to do when a church faces this kind of situation is for leaders to begin to have committee meetings and often to vote on a decision. But we knew from the start that Jesus wanted us to build a place where He could receive glory through transformed lives of people who lived in dependency upon Him. Jesus taught that as He was in the world, doing only what He saw the Father do, so He has sent us into the world to live in that kind of intimate relationship with Him (see John 5:19; 17:18).

We were still very young in our pursuit of our goal to live out the commandments of Jesus, but we had learned that the only way we could hope to fulfill that goal was to seek Him continually in prayer. There we would receive His instructions about how this vision should unfold. In order to do that, we had to lay down our opinions and personal ideas of what we should do. Our hope was in the promises of God: "Evil men understand not judgment: but they that seek the Lord understand all things" (Prov. 28:5).

We took seriously the teaching of the apostle Paul: "For as many as are led by the Spirit of God, they are the sons of God" (Rom. 8:14). We were careful not to attribute to God what some "leader" among us would decide was a good idea. Besides that, our ministry was so young that we didn't know who the leaders were yet. The overwhelming scope of what we were about kept us living in utter dependency on God, waiting to hear Him say, "...This is the way, walk ye in it..." (Isa. 30:21).

Out of a very intimate acquaintance with D.L. Moody, I wish to testify that he was a far greater pray-er than he was preacher. He knew the way to bring to pass anything that needed to be brought to pass. He knew and believed in the deepest depths of his soul that nothing was too hard for the Lord, and that prayer could do anything that God could do.

—R. A. Torrey[1]

CHAPTER 9

MOVING FORWARD...AGAIN

ONE SATURDAY MORNING, AS I was brushing my teeth, the Holy Spirit spoke very clearly to me and said, "The new sanctuary will resemble a combination of a house and a barn." When He spoke, I had a very clear vision of the building in my mind. Laminated beams set on concrete and rising twenty-eight feet at the apex made the perfect shape of a barn roof—simple, and at the same time beautiful and functional.

This design is not something I would have imagined. When I drive by the typical, white country churches, with their lovely steeples, that dot our beautiful northeast Tennessee hills, I tell my friends, "That is what I thought our church would be like." Yet the Holy Spirit spoke something very different to me. (Its attractive uniqueness has prompted several pastors who have visited to request the plans for our sanctuary for their use.)

While I was preaching the next morning, I shared the vision with the people. When I did, I received a clear impression to "do it now." After service that morning, we went outside and broke ground for the new sanctuary. We still have a photograph showing our congregation joyfully applauding as John and I turned over the first shovel of dirt on the portion of our property where the new sanctuary would be constructed.

Being led by the Spirit is a real adventure. I love the way He works. It is not complicated. Just tell Him your need. Get the plan. Work the plan. During the last four decades, many people have observed the beauty of our exquisitely landscaped property with its unique sanctuary design, our adjoining subdivision, and the educational and conference center facilities. Some have asked, "Did you have a master plan for the development of your property?" My simple, sincere response has been, "No, but we listened intently to the Master as He revealed His plan."

LEARNING THE VALUE OF MENTORS

Before the inception of Shekinah Church, as I mentioned, I had pursued theological studies for three years at a local Bible college. During that time, the vision God had given us was taking shape, and its rapid unfolding was sometimes overwhelming. We never dreamed of the scope of God's destiny for our lives. It seemed every time we were about to catch our breath, we were thrust into a new phase of the vision by the leading of the Holy Spirit. I found it necessary to withdraw from my formal studies shortly before graduation to give my time to the work at hand.

As I discussed, just three years after we had begun the work, we found ourselves planning the dedication of our second sanctuary. The congregation was growing as people were getting saved and embracing the vision God had given us. The demands of ministering to them increasingly required more of my time.

Still, I felt unprepared for the task I had been given in facing the challenges of pastoring. In prayer, the Holy Spirit showed me that I should look for "spiritual covering." I needed to find mature, seasoned ministers who would mentor me with the godly wisdom they had received through their experience as pastors.

A *mentor* is defined as a trusted counselor, guide, or tutor. There are numerous biblical examples of godly leaders who mentored young men and women to become godly leaders in their own right. For example,

Moses mentored Joshua, Elijah mentored Elisha, Jesus mentored Peter, and Paul mentored Timothy. Aquila and Priscilla, co-laborers with Paul, are recorded to have mentored Apollos, an eloquent teacher of the Scriptures, guiding him into "the way of God more perfectly" (Acts 18:26).

It is safe to conclude that, without the valuable wisdom of mentors, these upcoming leaders would have had difficulty fulfilling the purposes of God for their lives. I learned that these relationships are imperative for spiritual protection and for helping us grow as leaders to greater spiritual maturity. Only God knows how many pitfalls I have probably avoided by pursuing the counsel of mature ministers.

The late Dr. Judson Cornwall was an acclaimed pastor, author, and internationally esteemed "pastor to pastors." Until his death a few years ago, Judson (he insisted I call him by his first name) ministered faithfully for over three decades in our Ministers' Conferences. Our congregation loved Judson and his beloved wife, Eleanor, for their spiritual contribution to so many lives. Judson became a "spiritual father" for our church and one of my first personal mentors.

He was always available to me by telephone or e-mail, speaking into my personal and pastoral life from the wisdom he had gained through over fifty years of walking with God in ministry. There are some things we can only gain through these personal relationships; reading a book is not the same as being mentored by godly men and women.

It also occurred to me that I should pursue ordination with a reputable ministerial fellowship to assure proper credentialing. In that process, the Holy Spirit led me to some like-minded ministers. They embraced the vision they saw in our ministry and sincerely wanted to help us in any way they could.

Pastors John and Anne Gimenez, founders of Rock Church International in Virginia Beach, Virginia, were among those who prayed for me in the biblical pattern of the "laying on of hands" (see 2 Tim. 1:6). They acknowledged the call of God on my life and became lifelong friends and partners whose input I greatly value.

Again, I was reminded of the Scripture that declares, "...Not many mighty, not many noble are called" (I Cor. I:26). I learned that John Gimenez was a former drug addict, and his wife, Anne, was a woman evangelist saved in a T.L. Osborne service. I was simply a former corporation secretary. We were all just ordinary people who had had powerful, life-changing encounters with God. What sweet fellowship we enjoyed with these and other like-minded ministers whose lives were totally committed to simply being obedient to the "heavenly vision."

WELCOME ENCOURAGEMENT

I searched the Scriptures daily as I pursued my devotional relationship with the Holy Spirit. Many times I poured out my heart to Him about my misgivings, sense of inadequacy, and the current challenges I was facing. During the time I spent in His Word, I learned to take great comfort in Jesus' promises. For example, He declared to His disciples that *He* would build His Church:

> *And I say also unto thee, That thou art Peter, and upon this rock I will build my church; and the gates of hell shall not prevail against it* (Matthew 16:18).

The truth that Jesus will build His Church means to me that my responsibility is to pray to receive His direction and obey His instructions. His responsibility is to supply every need required for the task. As the Holy Spirit led me to pray, He was doing His part to bring everything in order. So that I would not become anxious, He gave John and me a surprise confirmation through a veteran minister known to be a reputable prophet.

We were still in the earliest stage of developing our property and constructing our buildings, and we had only a small congregation working with us. John and I went for a visit to the church in Virginia Beach, pastored by our friends, John and Anne Gimenez. It turned out to be a fortuitous visit, indeed.

We were entirely incognito in the congregation while Prophet David Schoch was ministering. We had not been introduced. Suddenly, he interrupted his message to point to my husband and me, and he began to speak to us personally in an authoritative, yet comforting, voice. I will never forget his words:

> I have a word for that young couple standing near the drummer boy. You have begun a work that is very unusual. It is a church, but more than a church. You have land and buildings...it is more like a community. And the Lord wants you to know that when you return to your charge you will find that He is sending responsible people to help with your ministry. You will find that He has gone before you to prepare for every need. It's going to be a new day for you from this moment.

That prophetic word of encouragement began to be fulfilled shortly after we returned to our home, and it has continued to be true to this day. God sent professional people who embraced the vision, helping with their skills and financial resources, as well as with their commitment to prayer and to living the commandments of Jesus.

From that time, Prophet David Shoch and his wife, Audeen, became personal friends who ministered with us in conferences and mentored us. We grew to deeply appreciate the accurate, godly prophetic ministry of David Schoch that edified our lives and ministry. Some in our congregation have described his godly character as liquid love flowing over every life he touched, bringing the healing power of God to them.

ESTABLISHING A CONFERENCE CENTER

Early in our relationship, Judson Cornwall shared with me a burden he had for pastors to be exposed to fervent corporate prayer, dynamic worship, and committed lives that were lived sacrificially and dedicated to fulfilling God's will. Everywhere he ministered, he taught these biblical truths for establishing a godly lifestyle that reflect God's commands for His Church. He wrote about them in his more than fifty published books.

Now he saw them being lived out in the prayerful lifestyle of our congregation as we pursued the vision God had given us. Judson wanted pastors to experience these spiritual realities in a "local church" setting. His burden became an integral part of the unfolding of our vision.

As I prayed about it with others, we agreed with Judson's burden that we should offer to host an annual conference at Shekinah for ministers. As a result, we hosted our first ministers' conference in 1978. From that moment to this day, we have dedicated our facilities for the purpose of training and empowering leaders to minister under the anointing of the Holy Spirit and to lead their people into prayer, worship, and a lifestyle of total commitment to God.

Since that time, we have continued to host several ministers' conferences annually. God has brought many well-known Christian leaders and conference speakers from around the world to share their wisdom. They have inspired and equipped Christian leaders and pastors from across our nation and other nations as well.

We have constantly been amazed that God has sent to us powerful ministries from our nation like Tommy Tenney, John Kilpatrick, Leonard Fox, Dr. Fuchsia Pickett, Dutch Sheets, and many others. From the nations, we have been delighted to receive ministry from Sunday Adelaja of the Ukraine, Heidi Baker of Mozambique, Bishop Duncan-Williams and Prophet Victor Boateng of Ghana, Dr. Ernest Komanapalli of India, Myles Munroe of the Bahamas, Carlos Annacondia of Argentina, Harold Caballeros of Guatemala, and many others.

People continually ask me how a little-known church in Blountville, Tennessee, is able to gain access to these prestigious ministries that often require large stadiums and conference centers to accommodate their audiences. I can only point to the faithfulness of Jesus, who is building His church as we maintain our commitment to our prayer lifestyle. As I seek His direction, He impresses me to contact particular ministries, inviting them to come—and they do.

Through these seasoned ministers, we have received God's unfolding revelation of His purposes in the earth for *now* as welcome, Holy Spirit-breathed direction. They have brought confirmation and inspiration regarding the purposes of God, not only for our church, but for many hundreds of pastors who have attended. And they have been invaluable in my husband John's life and in mine for encouragement, direction, and the mentorship they gave to us.

As the sons of Issachar, wise men of old who had understanding of the times (see 1 Chron. 12:32), these Christian leaders have their hearts tuned to the heart of God today. Receiving divine understanding of our times, they are able to equip the body of Christ to fulfill His purposes. Their messages have inspired new levels of faith, more fervency in prayer, and greater focus of our energies to establish the kingdom of God *His way.*

Ministry to the Nations

In 1978, the same year we hosted our first conference, John and I were invited to travel to India with Reverends John and Anne Gimenez. That first missions' trip to the nations was the beginning of the fulfillment of the prophetic word brought by Robert Thom in 1973.

The trip was not uneventful. I contracted the inevitable dysentery, and we experienced a life-threatening airplane incident in India when one of the plane's two engines failed. Yet, in spite of these challenges, we were able to initiate an outreach to India on that first missions' trip that has endured for decades. We worked with national ministries there to build a Bible school. We began to sink deep roots into the Christian church in India, with the goal of overthrowing the false religions and establishing knowledge of the true God in that oppressed nation.

As we continually sought God about our missions' effort in India, the Holy Spirit revealed to us year by year how we should be involved.

One year we had the opportunity to give a major portion of finances needed for the building of an eye clinic there. So many Indians would have lost their sight had there not been this provision for cataract surgery for the impoverished masses. Our missions in India were the beginning of our dedication to partnering with godly Christian leaders in many nations of the world.

MISSIONS—COMING AND GOING

Through the years, we have been able to take teams to minister in many nations. In turn, leaders from those nations have come to minister to us at Shekinah Church. As a result, networks of godly leadership relationships have been formed as we opened our hearts to the work of God around the world.

We learned that when the Holy Spirit is directing our footsteps, we will sometimes find ourselves walking "off the beaten path." We could not have imagined how the vision God had given us would unfold and enlarge or to what extent our lives would be transformed by just trying to "keep up" with it.

After all, who could have a mind to compare with the Holy Spirit, God's Great Intellect of the universe, one who promised to teach us all things and guide us into all truth. We were about to find out if we were willing to receive all the truth He had for us.

Many Christians backslide...They are unable to stand against the temptations of the world, or of their old nature. They strive to do their best to fight against sin, and to serve God, but they have not strength. They have never really grasped the secret: The Lord Jesus will every day from heaven continue His work in me. But on one condition—the soul must give Him time each day to impart His love and His grace. Time alone with the Lord Jesus each day is the indispensable condition of growth and power.

—Andrew Murray[1]

CHAPTER 10

SEEKING GOD FOR MIRACLES

FROM THE VERY BEGINNING OF my ministry, I knew that my message would involve teaching a restoration of truths that had been neglected by today's Church. The fact that the Holy Spirit had inspired me to live the commandments of Jesus in His "Sermon on the Mount" was an indication of that reality. I wasn't sure it could be done, but I was inspired to seek God to that end.

The more I studied Church history, the more I wondered what had happened to many of the great truths of the Church. The power of prevailing prayer, healing, and the miraculous intervention of God were so prevalent in the Church only a generation before.

As a child, I had heard of healing miracles in lives of people I knew. My mother, for example, had been healed of a tumor the size of an orange. After the church prayed for her, she returned to her doctor for examination. He told her that the tumor he had diagnosed was no longer there. She was also healed of other serious illnesses during her life in answer to prayer.

My father was an alcoholic, which involved a continual, heartbreaking cycle that disrupted our home. After he gave in to a drinking bout for several weeks, he would determine to become sober. That always resulted in terrible sickness. As a child, I was afraid he would die in this condition.

I remember one of these times particularly when, in tears, my father asked my mother if she would call "her preacher" to pray. I understood even as a child that he was not *his* preacher because my father didn't go to church. Mother called her preacher, and I witnessed the miracle-working power of God that day as my father was instantly healed when the preacher prayed for him.

When he came out of his bedroom, dressed and smiling broadly, I said, "Daddy you look so different." His response to me was, "That shows what the Lord can do for you." Even as a child, I wondered how we could have survived without the hope of receiving help from God. Somehow I knew that our problems were much too big for us to solve without Him.

MIRACLES HAVE GONE BEFORE

The truth that God still works miracles today desperately needs to be restored to much of the Church. I read that in the Azusa Street Pentecostal Outpouring in Los Angeles there were documented healings and miracles of every description. During that great revival, which historians concur was happening worldwide, powerful ministries of healing were birthed.

Men and women, such as Smith Wigglesworth, Aimee Semple Mcpherson, John G. Lake, Stanley Frodsham, and others, birthed many churches that embraced the miraculous power of God. They not only experienced salvation, but miracles of healing as well. The newspapers of the day published front-page headlines of documented healings and miracles happening in these churches.

Our friend, the late Prophet David Schoch, was a boy when his parents hosted Smith Wigglesworth as a guest in their California home. David related incidents of the miraculous power of God that he remembers witnessing in Wigglesworth's meetings. A seasoned minister himself, you could still sense the awe in his voice when he recalled the power of God that he had experienced as a child in those meetings.

Arthur Burt of Wales, now ninety-eight years of age, was a co-worker with Smith Wigglesworth. He also witnessed the power of God to heal and perform miracles. He has ministered at Shekinah several times, teaching the Word in great simplicity with his heavy Welsh brogue. Yet, he reveals a profound depth of genuine relationship with the Holy Spirit. His ministry has impacted the lives of our congregation. In true humility, he brings glory to God in all he does.

For example, when he is introduced as a man of God, his response is something like, "If you ask me who I am, I will tell you. I am nobody, and the message I bring today is that every "somebody" will have to become nobody. We must lose our identity in the body of Christ, because Father will not give His glory to anybody but Christ."[2]

As I studied powerful ministries of a generation ago and beyond, I learned that not only individuals, but also communities and entire cities were transformed by the miraculous power of God. The more I read, the more I developed a strong desire to see God's miracle power in the Church today.

FAITH FOR MIRACLES—TODAY

The simple, biblical definition of *miracle*, which is translated from the word *semeion* in the Greek, is "a sign, i.e. an unusual occurrence, transcending the common course of nature"[3] In other words, when there is a need for provision or healing or anything that God's Word promises, we can ask for a miracle. God's answer transcends the natural limitations of our situations. He wants us to believe Him for the miracles we need today.

Jesus promised that we could live an abundant life (see John 10:10). He said that if we would seek first the kingdom of God and His righteousness, everything we needed would be provided for us (see Matt. 6:33). He insisted that we not be anxious for anything; that does not reflect the peace He came to give us as the Prince of Peace. He wants to supernaturally, abundantly provide all we need to live the life He has chosen us to live.

Every time Jesus commissioned and sent disciples out, whether it was the twelve or the seventy (see Matt. 10:8; Luke 10:1), He gave these same three commands: Preach the gospel, heal the sick, cast out devils. In the book of Acts, we find that the phenomena of healing the sick and casting out devils, as well as the working of miracles (as in Peter's release from prison), continued as a way of life for the followers of Jesus.

And the apostle Paul included gifts of healings and working of miracles in the biblical list of supernatural endowments of the Holy Spirit (see I Cor. 12:28). I began to see throughout the Scriptures that God intended for healings, signs, wonders, and miracles to be experienced in our daily lives.

There is no biblical record that supports the idea of any cessation of these supernatural provisions for the body of Christ. It was meant to be a part of the abundant life Jesus came to bring all believers for all time:

> *The thief cometh not, but for to steal, and to kill, and to destroy: I am come that they might have life, and that they might have it more abundantly* (John 10:10).

I am aware that some theologians teach that miracles ceased after the canon of Scripture was completed. It seems a stretch for us to determine which teachings of the New Testament to carry forward and which to leave behind. I believe it is a safer theological position to acknowledge the plan of God for our supernatural empowerment to bring His purposes to earth through His miraculous intervention.

Certainly, beginning with our salvation, miracles should define the believer's relationship with God. The greatest miracle you can experience is to become alive to God after being "dead in trespasses and sins" (Eph. 2:1). If miracles ceased at some point in history, there would be no hope for people today to be reconciled to God and have their sins forgiven. Salvation, being truly born again by the Spirit, requires the miraculous intervention of God.

Jesus included miracles of healing and deliverance in His Great Commission. They are part of His mandate for all believers to preach the gospel:

> *And he said unto them, Go ye into all the world, and preach the gospel to every creature. He that believeth and is baptized shall be saved; but he that believeth not shall be damned. And these signs shall follow them that believe; In my name shall they cast out devils; they shall speak with new tongues; .They shall take up serpents; and if they drink any deadly thing, it shall not hurt them; they shall lay hands on the sick, and they shall recover* (Mark 16:15-18).

To experience healings and miracles, as the Scriptures teach, we need to understand how to pray for these things. It seems that for some it is easier to change their "theology" to *exclude* miracles than it is to commit to seeking God *until* the miracles happen. As a church, we have committed our lives to believing prayer to see the power of God bring the miracles we need.

MIRACLES ARE WONDERFUL

We were made acutely aware of the need for believing prayer during our first trip to India. John and I and our team had to fly in a small plane from one part of India to another. During the flight, one of the two engines malfunctioned. The pilot announced, "We are returning to Hyderabad because of technical difficulties." I noticed the flight attendant became suddenly pale and began returning all our trays to their locked position, demanding, "Check your seatbelts immediately."

Then the cabins lights failed and the air conditioning system ceased to work. The plane became very warm. No one said a word. The plane's engine could no longer be heard. In that moment, I learned that His faithfulness reaches to the clouds (see Ps. 36:5).

As we approached the airport in Hyderabad, we heard the landing gear engage. When our plane touched down everyone cheered.

Then we learned that the same thing had happened a week previously on the same type of plane. Unfortunately, that malfunctioning engine had caught fire and the plane had crashed. We knew we had experienced a miracle. When we entered the terminal, our team knelt down together and thanked our God. Through tears of joy, we quoted together the wonderful promise of God we had experienced:

For he shall give his angels charge over thee, to keep thee in all thy ways. They shall bear thee up in their hands, lest thou dash thy foot against a stone (Psalm 91:11-12).

Not until we returned home and were giving testimony to the faithfulness of God did we learn the rest of the story. Ann, my personal intercessor, had a dream that was so startling it awakened her. In her dream, a small plane burst into flames and crashed into the ocean. As she sensed the great danger, she knelt down and began to intercede fervently for the safety of that plane.

She cried out desperately for God to intervene and spare the destruction of that plane and its passengers. He heard and answered her cry. We compared the time of her dream with the time of our crisis in India, and they coincided.

Can we even imagine how many horrible accidents are avoided and how many lives are saved through a faithful intercessor's prayers? Jesus warned us that the thief comes to steal, to kill, and to destroy (see John 10:10). We must be alert and abort the enemy's plans by committing our lives to believing prayer to receive God's miracles in our lives. Only personal devotion to consistent prayer can make us sensitive to the Holy Spirit as Ann was that night.

BELIEVING GOD FOR HEALING

The Holy Spirit taught me to believe God for divine healing when serious physical needs presented themselves. As a body of believers, we simply believed the Word of God and took Jesus as our Healer. We learned that one of the Old Testament names of God is Jehovah-Rophe, "I am the Lord that healeth thee." When God spoke His name to Moses as our Healer, He was referring to physical healing (see Exod. 15:25-26).

When Jesus came, He revealed the heart of the Father to bring healing to all who are oppressed:

> ...*God anointed Jesus of Nazareth with the Holy Ghost and with power: who went about doing good, and healing all that were oppressed of the devil; for God was with him* (Acts 10:38).

I have learned from the Scriptures that Jesus heals people in many different ways. That is why it is so important to listen to the Holy Spirit as we pray and seek to help people receive a miracle from God. In the Scriptures, we read that Jesus sometimes rebuked a demon to release healing to a person; at other times, He told people their faith had brought their healing; on one occasion, he made clay of His spittle, placed it on a blind man's eyes, and told him to go wash in a pool to receive his healing.

In our ministry, we are seeking to follow the instructions of the Holy Spirit, which of course must agree with the written Word. We have seen many people healed supernaturally through the years. Sometimes the Holy Spirit would convict people of unforgiveness in their lives. When they made things right, healing would come. This follows the pattern of the New Testament exhortation:

> *Confess your faults one to another, and pray one for another, that ye may be healed. The effectual fervent prayer of a righteous man availeth much* (James 5:16).

In that same passage, the apostle James gave another biblical injunction regarding divine healing, instructing believers to:

> ...*call for the elders of the church; and let them pray over him, anointing him with oil in the name of the Lord: and the prayer of faith shall save the sick,*

and the Lord shall raise him up; and if he have committed sins, they shall be forgiven him (James 5:14-15).

We appreciate what doctors and medicine can do, and we believe that God can use them to alleviate suffering. We also know that Jesus heals supernaturally. And when doctors have no answers, Jesus becomes our only recourse to defeat the destructive power of disease.

Like the woman who had the issue of blood and spent all she had on doctors, growing only worse, we must learn to press through "the crowd" and touch the hem of Jesus' garment in faith to receive supernatural healing (see Luke 8:44-47). Jesus did not condemn her for her act; He commended her for her faith. Desperately crying out to God for healing is the surest way to bring the Healer into your situation.

As we endeavor to walk in these truths for today, our relationship with God becomes the focus of our entire lives. In cultivating intimate relationship with Him through prayer, our hearts are enlarged to seek Him more and more. And He has promised that when we seek Him with all our hearts, we will find Him.

When the Holy Spirit reveals Jesus to us, as He has promised to do, all we can do is bow in worship in His presence. In this way, the Holy Spirit is restoring the principle of worship in spirit and truth (see John 4) to the Church that seeks Him diligently.

Prayer should not be regarded "as a duty which must be performed," but rather as a privilege to be enjoyed, a rare delight that is always revealing some new beauty.

—*E.M. Bounds*[1]

CULTIVATING A WORSHIPING HEART

Shortly after I was born again, the Holy Spirit introduced me to the wonderful reality of praise and worship. Spontaneously, I began to praise God simply because He was amazing me so often by the things He was doing in our lives. It just seemed natural to praise Him. As I studied the Scriptures, I learned that praise is the biblical response to the greatness and the faithfulness of God in our lives.

When our ministry first began, we did not have any musical instruments in the church, not even a keyboard. Our voices were the instruments we used to praise God. In our zeal and love for God, they were all that was needed to take us into the presence of God. We gathered together and poured our hearts out in expressing our love for Him.

During those early years, a seasoned pastor from Seattle, Washington, who had experienced revivals of praise and worship in previous decades, came to minister for us. Amazed at the vibrant praise and worship we were experiencing corporately, she asked, "How have you come so far in worship without anyone to lead you?"

I responded simply, "The Holy Spirit led us to the Scriptures that instructed us about praise and worship."

After the Lord led us into the revival of prayer in 1980 (which I talk about in Chapter 12), we entered into depths of praise and worship that many pastors who came to visit had not experienced at that time.

Often, our prayers were interspersed with songs of victorious praise or songs of worship and adoration.

Afterward, there was always greater empowerment to pray as our faith was lifted through praise and worship. During those faith-filled meetings, many new songs were given spontaneously. Some have traveled around the world and are still being sung in churches. We were truly enjoying the atmosphere of heaven through corporate praise and worship.

Judson Cornwall recognized the genuineness of our corporate praise and worship in hearts surrendered to God and anointed to serve Him. That was when he suggested we begin to host Worship Conferences so that pastors and worship leaders could learn what the Holy Spirit had taught us about entering into the presence of God through worship.

THE POWER OF CORPORATE PRAISE

As we learn to cultivate praise and worship in our personal devotional lives, we can become a part of the powerful expression of corporate worship. The Scriptures record examples of the power of praise alone conquering the enemy.

King Jehoshaphat called on God in fervent prayer when a great multitude arrayed themselves in battle against his nation. The Lord spoke to him through a Levite, saying that God was with them and that they would not need to fight in this battle. They were to simply stand still and see the deliverance of the Lord. Then the King fell before the Lord, worshiping Him. After that:

> *...he appointed singers unto the Lord, and that should praise the beauty of holiness, as they went out before the army, and to say, Praise the Lord; for his mercy endureth for ever. And when they began to sing and to praise, the Lord set ambushments against the children of Ammon, Moab, and mount Seir; which were come against Judah; and they were smitten* (2 Chronicles 20:14-22).

When Paul and Silas were in stocks in prison, at midnight they began to lift their voices in praise to God. They experienced a supernatural deliverance from prison and gained the salvation of souls there as a result of their determination to praise God no matter their circumstances.

At Shekinah, we consider corporate worship to be part of our DNA as a church. And we were pleasantly surprised when two ministers who came recently from the nations to minister to us asked us to extend our worship time. Heidi Baker of Mozambique and Prophet Victor Boateng of Ghana revealed their personal dependency on the presence of God released in corporate worship. They worship first to prepare their own hearts to begin to minister to the congregation.

Praise and worship are the atmosphere of heaven. Jesus said we must worship Him in spirit and in truth (see John 4:23). Your spirit is designed by God to dominate your soul (mind, will, and emotions). When you yield to the Holy Spirit, who resides in your spirit, He empowers you to take dominion over your "sin nature."

Then your spirit is set free to enjoy God through praise and worship. In that way, your life is empowered to walk in the Spirit and be led by the Spirit. As you cultivate a worshiping heart, you will begin to enjoy the atmosphere of heaven; you will learn to dwell in the presence of God.

HEAVENLY ATMOSPHERE

In the Scriptures, when the curtain is pulled back to give us a glimpse of life in heaven, we always see the residents of heaven engaged in worship. Perhaps there are other activities happening there, but it is clear that all is done in an atmosphere of continual praise and worship.

For example, on one occasion we are introduced to angels who are tending vials filled with the prayers of the saints; they are mixing heavenly incense with the prayers.

Then another angel, having a golden censer, came and stood at the altar. He was given much incense that he should offer it with the prayers of all the saints upon the golden altar, which was before the throne. And the smoke of the incense, with the prayers of the saints, ascended before God from the angel's hand. Then the angel took the censer, filled it with fire from the altar, and threw it to the earth. And there were noises, thunderings, lightnings, and an earthquake (Revelation 8:3-5 NKJV).

On another occasion, the Scriptures show us the elders falling down before the throne of God to worship Him (see Rev. 5:6-10). Everyone had a harp and a vial, representing worship and prayer mixed together. According to the Scriptures, there is continual prayer and worship around the throne of God.

Throughout the Old and New Testaments, praise and worship are presented as the atmosphere of heaven. The more we cultivate this atmosphere in our personal lives and in our churches, the more of heaven we will experience. God chooses to inhabit the praises of His people (see Ps. 22:3). The Scriptures promise that when we bring the presence of God into our lives through worship, our days will become as days of heaven on earth (see Deut. 11:21).

The Scriptures declare that the kingdom of God is righteousness, peace, and joy in the Holy Ghost (see Rom. 14:17). Those are characteristics of heaven's atmosphere. It is true that Jesus said we would have tribulation in the world (see John 16:33). Yet, He also promised to give us His peace and joy.

A.B. Simpson, whose ministry to the immigrants in New York City during the 19th century led to the founding of the Christian and Missionary Alliance (circa 1873), explained this paradox of experiencing heaven's joy even in tribulation. In his daily devotional, *Days of Heaven On Earth,* he wrote:

There is a joy that springs spontaneously in the heart without any external or even rational cause. It is like an artesian fountain. It rejoices because it cannot help it. It is the glory of God; it is the heart of Christ; it is the joy divine of which He says, *These things have I spoken unto you, that my joy might remain in you, and that your joy might be full* (John 15:11). And your joy no man can take from you.

Those who possess this fountain are not discouraged by surrounding circumstances. Rather, they are often surprised at the deep, sweet gladness that comes without apparent cause—a joy that frequently is strongest when everything in their condition and circumstances would tend to fill them with sorrow and depression.[2]

Cultivating a worshiping heart results in lives lived in the atmosphere of heaven.

PRAISE IS A CHOICE

After I was saved, I began to learn that I could choose to praise God and release the power of God into my life. He wanted to set me free from oppressive or depressing thoughts and feelings related to my emotional responses. I began to understand that I could praise the Lord no matter how I felt. The psalmist commanded his soul to praise the Lord: "Bless the Lord O my soul: and all that is within me, bless his holy name" (Ps. 103:1).

My pastor, the late Dr. Judson Cornwall, who mentored me in the area of praise and worship, wrote several books on the subject. He told me I could trade the spirit of heaviness for the garment of praise; it was my choice. Sometimes, when I forget this principle and endeavor to plod through my praying in heaviness, the Holy Spirit faithfully reminds me what He taught me through my beloved pastor. Jesus told us that the Holy Spirit would guide us into all truth (see John 16:13). Many times my gratitude overflows as I find myself returning to the truth He taught me about the power of praise.

The New Testament exhorts believers to "...be filled with the Spirit, speaking to yourselves in psalms and hymns and spiritual songs…" (Eph. 5:18-19). From the beginning, the Holy Spirit taught us as a church the truth of praise and worship. We became aware of the predominant place worship was to have in our individual lives and corporately as a church.

During the last four decades, as praise and worship has become pre-eminent among many worshiping congregations, the focus of some has strayed. Instead of focusing on God, they have focused on the kind of instruments, the use of guitars, drums, keyboards, and various styles of music. The power of worship is released as we focus on God, praising Him and exalting His greatness and majesty.

In my devotional time, I cannot imagine prayer without praise and worship. As I lift my voice in prayer, sometimes the Holy Spirit will lead me to sing my prayers. Psalm 81:1 tells us to "Sing aloud to God our strength…." Singing is mentioned 287 times in the Bible. In the tabernacle of David, he hired hundreds of people to sing day and night in the presence of the Ark of God. God made us to sing and to praise Him.

The Scriptures confirm the importance of praise, using seven different Hebrew words to describe different facets of its expression (see Appendix A). Incorporating various forms of praise in your personal devotional life and in corporate worship will honor God and brings His power and blessing into your life.

BENEFITS OF PRAISE AND WORSHIP

The spiritual victories that I have shared with you in my life and ministry are results of living a life of prayer. That prayer lifestyle involves these biblical patterns of praise and worship. It is not possible in these pages to outline all the benefits of cultivating a heart of worship. However, listing a few of them will be helpful to inspire you to focus on living a life characterized by praise and worship.

1. Praise drives back the enemy.

In the story of Jehoshaphat's crisis, we saw that he cried out to God for help. God fought the battle for them. All the people had to do was to sing and praise and then pick up the spoils after the battle was over.

The psalmist declared that praise is a weapon for the people of God:

Let the high praises of God be in their mouth, and a two-edged sword in their hand; to execute vengeance upon the heathen, and punishments upon the people; to bind their kings with chains, and their nobles with fetters of iron; to execute upon them the judgment written: this honour have all his saints. Praise ye the Lord (Psalm 149:6-9).

The Holy Spirit taught me that the high praises of God in my mouth would be a tool of authority that God would use to execute vengeance and judgment. *High praises* means praising God with strong faith and conviction regarding who He is and what He will do.

2. Joy accompanies praise.

The Scriptures link praise with a joyful heart, and it is impossible to focus on God and exalt Him without experiencing the joy His presence brings. Joy characterizes His kingdom:

To appoint unto them that mourn in Zion, to give unto them beauty for ashes, the oil of joy for mourning, the garment of praise for the spirit of heaviness; that they might be called trees of righteousness, the planting of the Lord, that he might be glorified (Isaiah 61:3).

Thou wilt shew me the path of life: in thy presence is fulness of joy; at thy right hand there are pleasures for evermore (Psalm 16:11).

3. Renew your strength.

When weariness overwhelms you, whether physical, emotional, or even spiritual, check your praise quotient; when you choose to enter His presence through praise, you will find His rest:

And [God] *said, My presence shall go with thee, and I will give thee rest* (Exodus 33:14).

Come unto me, all ye that labour and are heavy laden, and I will give you rest (Matthew 11:28).

4. Praise paves the way for miracles.

A Canaanite woman came to Jesus and extolled Him as Lord and the Son of David. And she cried to Him to deliver her daughter, who was vexed with a devil. At first, Jesus remonstrated that He was sent to the house of Israel.

How beautiful is this poignant scene recorded in the Scriptures of this desperate mother: "Then came she and worshiped him, saying, Lord, help me" (Matt. 15:25). Jesus relented and commended her for her great faith, restoring her daughter's health completely (see Matt 15:28).

PRAISE VERSUS WORSHIP

Much has been written to distinguish *praise*, as a biblical expression of our love to God, from *worship*, described as a response to His manifest presence. Praise and worship are so intertwined that it is not easy to delineate between them. Yet, we can note some distinctions that can be helpful to cultivating a worshiping heart. Put simply:

- Praise is initiated by us. Worship is our response to God's presence.

- Praise is us building a house for God. Worship is God moving in.

Praise to God acknowledges who He is, extols His divine attributes, gives thanks for His mighty acts, and humbles our hearts as creatures before our Creator. The psalmist declared that we are to enter His gates with thanksgiving and come into His courts with praise (see Ps. 100:4). Coming into His presence, we are to bring with us an offering of the fruit of our lips, which is our praise (see Heb. 13:15).

Worship, as revealed in the Scriptures, is a heart response to His wonderful, manifest presence. In both Old and New Testaments, when people encountered the Lord personally, their automatic response was to bow or fall before Him in worship. A heart bowed in worship is expressing the love and adoration it feels as a result of this personal encounter with Divine Love.

As you spend time with the Lord, it is appropriate to begin with praise rather than your "want list." As you express your gratitude for who He is and what He has done for you, faith rises in your heart to believe Him for what you need presently. You are cleansed from any "whining" or pity or other negative attitudes when you dwell in praise.

And when you sense His nearness, the only appropriate response is to bow in worship as a creature before your Creator, God, Savior, Lord, and Master. That is when your heart is most satisfied, most free, and you are aware of your acceptance in the beloved (see Eph. 1:6). Cultivating a heart of worship will truly make your days as days of heaven on earth (see Deut. 11:21).

As I mentioned, our praise and worship as a congregation was very simple during those first years of establishing Shekinah Church. Yet our hearts were seeking God and worshiping Him sincerely; we wanted to know Him in a greater way. He heard our cry and surprised us with a powerful visitation that propelled us forward into our destiny as a worshiping church.

There has never been a spirit awakening in any country or locality that did not begin in united prayer.

—*A.T. Pierson*[1]

CHAPTER 12

SURPRISED BY THE HOLY SPIRIT

IT WAS AN ORDINARY FEBRUARY morning in 1980—until it became the day that changed my life and the life of our church. It is an understatement to say that we would never be the same again. During the previous seven years, we had taken great strides forward in building a place where we could live the commandments of Jesus.

God had sovereignly sent people to visit our services who were also looking for reality of relationship with God. They readily joined with us in our vision to live the Sermon on the Mount and help hurting people. Our growing congregation had made themselves available in their spare time to help develop our property and build the facilities we needed.

Through their tireless commitment, our lovely sanctuary and offices were soon completed. We began work on an adjoining subdivision where some of us had purchased lots to build our own homes. In addition, we had remodeled the old farmhouse to serve as expanded educational facilities. And we had completed a lovely guesthouse that would house some of our guests who attended our conferences.

There was so much building and developing of the property that we began to see our need for a full-time director and administrator. My husband, John, made the decision to resign from his work as research chemist to fulfill that need. Now, literally, God had gotten His man into the land—permanently. It was quite a step of faith for us, financially and in every other way.

Yet as we gave ourselves to the daily work of the ministry, we were convinced that we were totally involved in our eternal destiny. We continued to seek God earnestly, both privately and corporately, desiring to please God in the place He had chosen for us to build. What happened next would make the challenges we had faced during the past seven years look like child's play.

A HOLY SPIRIT-BREATHED REVIVAL

That February morning, I preached a message called "Acts Revival" in which I referenced the account of what happened on the Day of Pentecost (see Acts 2). I read Jesus' command to His disciples:

...but wait for the promise of the Father, which...ye have heard of me. For John truly baptized with water; but ye shall be baptized with the Holy Ghost not many days hence (Acts 1:4-5).

As I preached, I recounted what had happened when the Day of Pentecost came. A sound from heaven like a mighty rushing wind filled the house, and tongues of fire sat on the heads of everyone waiting in that upper room (see Acts 2:3). One hundred and twenty people experienced that powerful event, which the Scripture describes like this: "And they were all filled with the Holy Ghost, and began to speak with other tongues, as the Spirit gave them utterance" (Acts 2:4).

As I was simply recounting what had happened on the Day of Pentecost, the convicting presence of the Holy Spirit gripped the hearts of our congregation. They cried out to God to know His presence as those disciples had. As a result of this powerful response to the Word and the moving of the Holy Spirit, we decided to set aside the following week to pray together daily.

"Extra" Prayer Meetings

We planned to meet together, morning, afternoon, and evening, for an hour or so of prayer. We wanted to be available for whatever it was the Holy Spirit had begun in that Sunday morning service. So much for our plans. The Holy Spirit moved so powerfully in our hearts during that first morning prayer meeting that it ran into the afternoon prayer meeting, which ran into the evening meeting! We were in prayer all day, while people came and went as their work schedules demanded.

God melted our hearts in His powerful, felt presence as we poured out our love in worship before Him. The Holy Spirit convicted us of secret sins and brought us to deep repentance and wonderful cleansing. We simply waited on God and craved His presence that was filling our hearts with His love.

The Holy Spirit worked differently in every meeting, revealing different facets of the love of God. At times, He worked in hearts to evoke honest repentance; at other times, He gave new songs of praise and worship; sometimes revelations from the Word were shared that were a blessing to everyone. Each meeting was different, and no one wanted to miss out on what was happening. Our entire congregation, including our children, participated around their school and work schedules in these all-day prayer meetings that first week.

Some of the spontaneous songs of abandoned worship that were birthed during those prayer meetings became revival songs for the congregation. We compiled an entire songbook of these new songs and sang them in our Sunday services. Some have traveled around the world and can be heard today in worshiping congregations.

During this prayer revival, the Holy Spirit infused our hearts with a deep love for each other. Humbling ourselves to pray together, to repent and weep together, sharing our hearts before God, we were set free from pride, the fear of people, and many other bondages. The love of God was truly shed abroad in our hearts by the working of the Holy Ghost (see Rom. 5:5).

He also gave us a cry for the lost and for hurting people. He began to birth desires in our hearts for the ministry outreaches He had ordained for us. And He filled our hearts with faith to fulfill those divine missions. This powerful intensity of the Holy Spirit remained with us in daily corporate prayer meetings for three months—day and night.

After that, we gradually regained a "normal" lifestyle with scheduled prayer meetings several times a week, where we continued to enjoy the powerful, life-changing work of the Holy Spirit. That saturation presence of the Spirit of prayer continued in strength for an entire year among our congregation.

GREATER DEPENDENCY ON PRAYER

It was during our "prayer revival" that the Holy Spirit intensified His instruction to us in praying through the purposes of God—not just for our personal lives, but for our future as a church. Of course, we had been walking in the revealed will of God in establishing the place He had asked us to build for Him during the past seven years. And our lives were continually unfolding according to that heavenly vision.

But it didn't take long for everyone to realize that, on that February morning, when we were arrested by the presence of the Holy Spirit, we had entered a new dimension of prayer. The entire congregation was saturated with zeal for prayer and humbled in God's presence through repentance and cleansing.

As a result, we were ushered into a greater dependency on God in prayer and new dimensions of God's calling on our lives. New facets of the vision were birthed through prayer during those months of submitting to the intensity of His presence.

Now, thirty years later, we can point to this amazing visitation of the Holy Spirit as the catalyst for establishing outreach ministries around the world. These ministries would increase our dependency on our prayer lifestyle. They would engage our lives in the work of God for the foreseeable future. But more about that later.

Allowing the Expert to Do It

After the Holy Spirit came to us sovereignly in our prayer revival, I wondered how we could have walked with God for over a decade without knowing what He had just taught us in prayer. He revealed His supernatural power to take the striving and difficulty out of prayer, both personal and corporate. It seemed effortless just to wait in His presence and watch Him move among us supernaturally.

We acknowledge that we had received many miracles to date through prayer. Yet we were also aware of the futility of our own efforts to maintain a prayer lifestyle. Frankly, before this prayer revival, sometimes we dreaded going to our prayer meetings. At times it seemed no one wanted to pray. The meetings were lifeless, and we were relieved when they were over.

Children learn about new dimensions of life only when they mature enough to experience them; in the same way, we were learning about new dimensions of prayer as we experienced these life-changing encounters with the Holy Spirit. We found ourselves thrown on Him in new dependency, continuing to trust the Scriptures for His expert guidance in prayer:

> *Likewise the Spirit also helpeth our infirmities: for we know not what we should pray for as we ought: but the Spirit itself maketh intercession for us with groanings which cannot be uttered* (Romans 8:26).

As I have mentioned, this verse tells you that the Holy Spirit will actually help you to pray and to know *what* to pray, according to the will of God. It is awesome to think that He becomes both your Prayer Advisor as well as your expression in prayer.

When the apostle Paul said, "You don't know how to pray as you should" (see Rom. 8:26), he answered a lot of questions about why we have such a struggle in prayer. Too often we are praying as if we *know* something that Paul says *we don't know*. We don't know how to pray as we ought.

My husband is a mathematician. He understands mathematical concepts because of his education. When he begins to speak in terms of advanced math, I don't understand what he is saying. I'm not supposed to understand because that was never my field of study. If I have a need for advanced mathematic principles, I expect him to utilize them for me.

Similarly, the Holy Spirit knows everything about everything. He knows how we should pray. When we accept the truth that we do not know how we should pray, we should expect Him to do that for us. In our prayer revival, as we learned to be led by the Holy Spirit, we found that He prayed the will of God through us by His power. In repentance, revelation of the Word, desire for lost souls—it was the Holy Spirit Himself who initiated our prayers. There was no more intellectual striving to pray what we thought we should.

This is as God intended; it is what it means, in part, to be sons of God: "For as many as are led by the Spirit of God, they are the sons of God" (Rom. 8:14). We were learning how to be led by the Spirit of God into a new realm of prayer.

And we were entering a level of maturity that allowed us to experience His power of prayer in new dimensions. As the Holy Spirit continued to fill our hearts with zeal to pray, He taught us, day by day, how to pray corporately. In short, He taught us to become a praying church. In that learning process, we began to fulfill the mandate Jesus gave: "...Is it not written, My house shall be called a house of prayer for all nations?" (Mark 11:17 NKJV).

The one concern of the devil is to keep Christians from praying. He fears nothing from prayerless studies, prayerless work and prayerless religion. He laughs at our toil, mocks at our wisdom, but he trembles when we pray.

—Samuel Chadwick[1]

CHAPTER 13

LEARNING TO PRAY CORPORATELY

As I HAVE SAID, PRAYING in the Spirit and cultivating a prayer life-style were a priority for me and for our church from the beginning. As our congregation grew, we tried to have corporate prayer meetings, but we weren't very good at it. Before the Holy Spirit came to us in this powerful prayer visitation, our prayer meetings could be a real trial.

We would laughingly say to each other that our corporate prayer meetings were worse than dead. That was an understatement. We started using the picturesque terminology found in Jude to describe them: "twice dead, plucked up by the roots" (Jude 1:12).

When we tried to pray corporately before the revival, we experienced a variety of difficulties. In my book, *The Praying Church*,[2] I candidly discuss some of these very real hindrances that derail corporate praying (also see Appendix B). Pastors who have struggled to lead prayer meetings have especially appreciated my cataloguing of these difficulties, along with the solutions we found helpful.

In short, corporate prayer meetings have two strong enemies: the flesh and the devil. This reality prompted Charles Finney, the great revivalist, to say, "The devil has no conscience and the flesh has no sense. Together they can ruin any prayer meeting."[3]

No matter our sincere efforts to "have prayer meetings," the fact is that prayer is spiritual and must be orchestrated by the Spirit of God.

Charles Finney concluded, "The prayer meeting is the most difficult meeting of the church to sustain; and it should be because they are the most spiritual meetings of the church"[4]

We can perhaps preach interesting sermons without the Holy Spirit. We can conduct praise services without the Holy Spirit. But trying to pray without the supernatural aid of the Holy Spirit so exposes the deadness of the flesh that it becomes impossible even for the flesh to bear.

HOLY SPIRIT POWER TRANSCENDS
OUR NATURAL MINDS

During those months of revival when we were involved in continuous, Spirit-led praying, we felt as if we had entered a door into another spiritual realm. We learned with much more clarity that God created us, saved us, and called us to be spiritual beings first—overruling the "natural" self whose mind is hostile to God (see Rom. 8:7 NLT). We began to expect to live our lives entirely energized by the Spirit of God. Suddenly, we understood what the apostle Paul meant when he wrote:

> *But the natural man receiveth not the things of the Spirit of God: for they are foolishness unto him: neither can he know them, because they are spiritually discerned* (I Corinthians 2:14).

Even before the Holy Spirit came to us in this sovereign prayer revival, I had learned that the Holy Spirit is the divine Agent of true revival. Revival is so much more than a scheduled series of meetings with special speakers to encourage believers. It is the saturation presence of the Spirit of God doing His supernatural work, filling hearts with His love, and radically changing lives. As the Agent of revival, when the Holy Spirit is present, He changes people, and He changes otherwise impossible situations. He also comes as the Spirit of conviction to redeem us from hidden sin: "And when he is come, he will

reprove the world of sin, and of righteousness, and of judgment..."
(John 16:8).

HEARTFELT REPENTANCE

When the Holy Spirit convicts of sin, He creates a strong desire in the hearts of sinners and believers alike to repent. There is a longing to get things right with God and with other people against whom we have sinned.

I remember one young man in our congregation who began to recognize how much his sins had grieved the Lord. He was grieved at how he had failed the Lord after all He had done for him. During one of our corporate prayer meetings, he began to pour out his heart in prayer, to acknowledge his failure, and to ask God to forgive and cleanse him.

This man was a Christian; he was not repenting in order to become born again. Under the conviction of the Holy Spirit, he was seeing what John the Baptist had preached—that God called people to repent, not just of what they have done, but of who they have been:

> And now also the axe is laid unto the root of the trees: therefore every tree which bringeth not forth good fruit is hewn down, and cast into the fire (Matthew 3:10).

As the Holy Spirit convicted this man, the axe was laid to the root of his wicked thoughts and selfish desires. It was not condemnation he experienced, which just makes us feel bad about ourselves. He was truly convicted of sin, which gave him hope of being different when he made it right with God through heartfelt repentance.

There was a visitor in the meeting that night (there were many during those months) listening to this young man. A well-meaning Christian lady, she did not yet understand conviction that brought such contrition of heart. She went to this young man and said, "Son, if you are a Christian, Jesus has forgiven you; you don't need to cry and repent like this."

Lying prostrate on the floor, he struggled to a kneeling position and through his tears said with a quiet voice, "I appreciate your concern for me, lady, but I've just got to do this." Then he returned to pouring out His heart to God, thanking Him for His great love and compassion on his soul.

This young man became a leader and intercessor in the church, showing great sensitivity to anything in his life that would grieve the Holy Spirit. Without that convicting power of the Holy Spirit, he would not have understood that God wanted him to rid himself of sins not yet put under the blood of Jesus. He would not have known to "put off the old man and put on the new man" as the epistles clearly teach (see Eph. 4:22).

Such contrition of heart and compassion for each other we had never known. That only comes when the Holy Spirit is working to show God's great love that leads us to repentance:

> *Or despisest thou the riches of his goodness and forbearance and longsuffering; not knowing that the goodness of God leadeth thee to repentance?* (Romans 2:4)

One of the convincing proofs that the Holy Spirit, the Spirit of Love, was moving among us was that when we listened to others repent, we wept with them. And we rejoiced with them in their new-found freedom from sin and their joy of forgiveness. Often, the repentance of others made us aware of certain sins in our own hearts that we had not recognized. Then we in turn asked the Lord for cleansing. The love of God flowed like a river, breaking down all barriers of pride and shame and leading us into great liberty and deep love for one another.

THE SPIRIT OF PRAYER

We began to understand that the Holy Spirit was indeed the Spirit of prayer. In her classic trilogy, *The Holy Spirit's Work in You,* Dr. Fuchsia

Pickett discusses the seven divine offices of the Holy Spirit (see Appendix C). One of His offices is the Spirit of Supplication:

And I will pour upon the house of David, and upon the inhabitants of Jerusalem, the spirit of grace and of supplications... (Zechariah 12:10).

Fuchsia Pickett writes:

> We do not use the word *supplication* very often in our vocabulary today. Supplication is by definition "an entreaty, a humble earnest prayer in worship, a petition." In its broadest meaning, the word embraces the entire realm of prayer. As the Spirit of Supplication, the Holy Spirit executes the office of prayer, governing the communication department between our spirit and God...The Spirit of Supplication comes to establish us in a prayer relationship with God so we can commune freely with Him.[5]

What wonderful, supernatural help God has given us to pray. We must recognize how much we need the Holy Spirit to teach us to pray. The Holy Spirit working among us directs us, challenges us, and inspires us to real communication with God. He convicts us of sin and leads us to repentance, which gives us wonderful peace with God.

In gratitude for receiving the righteousness of God, we then begin to be filled with a desire to worship and adore our Savior and Lord. These truly spiritual experiences can only be initiated by the Holy Spirit, who is given to lead us into all truth:

Howbeit when he, the Spirit of truth, is come, he will guide you into all truth: for he shall not speak of himself; but whatsoever he shall hear, that shall he speak: and he will shew you things to come (John 16:13).

The Holy Spirit leads us into the wonderful truths of developing intimate relationship with God and living in the fulfillment of His promises. He also makes us aware of the terrible fact that God is coming to judge the world. He gives us a healthy fear of God, not wanting to displease Him. And He instills in us a deep compassion for others to know this wonderful salvation that we have received.

TRANSFORMED LIVES

During our prayer revival, as we opened our hearts to receive truth about ourselves, our sin, and the need for repentance, the Holy Spirit also revealed wonderful things about Himself. He filled us with His love for each other and for the lost. We learned to a greater measure the truth of what the apostle Paul declared: "...the love of God is shed abroad in our hearts by the Holy Ghost which is given unto us" (Rom. 5:5).

It is a fact that for several years after this powerful visitation of the Holy Spirit in our congregation, I did not hear one word of backbiting or negative speaking against brothers and sisters in the church. There was a deep joy among us when we gathered, a rejoicing at others' victories, and a compassion for each others' struggles.

As the Holy Spirit continued to teach us to pray, we were to discover His plans for our lives individually and as a church that we had never dreamed of. Life became a greater adventure than ever when He birthed the purposes of God, opening many doors of ministry that brought students and leaders alike from the nations and took us to the nations as well.

Prayer is the true genetic code of the church. We have received other mutant genes that have caused us to evolve away from God's true design for His body. Nothing that God is going to do will happen without prayer.

—Mahesh Chavda[1]

CHAPTER 14

THE POWER OF AGREEMENT

AS THE WEEKS AND MONTHS went by and we continued to experience Holy Ghost revival, the Spirit of God was teaching me to lead the corporate prayer meetings. Each was different and presented different challenges. Learning to be led by the Spirit is just that—learning. I was spending as much time in private prayer and waiting on God as I was in corporate gatherings, seeking wisdom to obey the Spirit of God.

As I mentioned, before revival, it seemed that often when a group of people gathered to pray, long silences between prayers became uncomfortable and awkward. Also, it seemed difficult to engage everyone to focus in prayer with the one who was praying aloud.

In my book, *The Praying Church*, I detail many lessons we learned about corporate prayer through this time. I want to mention one lesson we learned that can make or break a corporate prayer meeting. That is the need to learn to pray in agreement.

Jesus taught the tremendous power there is when just two people agree in prayer:

> *...if two of you shall agree on earth as touching any thing that they shall ask, it shall be done for them of my Father which is in heaven. For where two or three are gathered together in my name, there am I in the midst of them* (Matthew 18:19-20).

The Holy Spirit began to show me how to overcome the difficulty of awkward silence and lack of agreement. The Scriptures teach that praying in the Spirit builds up our inner person, strengthening us with His might (see Eph. 3:16). So I instructed our people that we should pray together in the Spirit, in tongues, at the beginning of the prayer meeting.

Then when we sense a liberty and unction to pray with the understanding, the Holy Spirit leads someone (perhaps in leadership) to pray a prayer that is the burden of God's heart. Others can stand in agreement with that prayer by saying things like "Amen," "Yes, Lord," or "I agree."

Then they begin praying prayers with the understanding in turn that help to carry that burden before God. They are agreeing with the first prayer and adding their voice to help lift that burden to the Lord. It is so exciting and life-giving to hear people pray verses of Scripture that help to lift that burden to God. There is a real sense that the corporate body is interceding together for the will of God.

Meanwhile, all are agreeing with these prayers and rejoicing that the Holy Spirit is leading us in a powerful way to establish the kingdom of God through prayer. I also learned that if we will pray softly in tongues, while others are leading in prayer, it is a wonderful way to express agreement. It also helps to keep our own spirits engaged in the spirit of prayer.

In my book, *The Praying Church*, I explain this divine dynamic of agreement in corporate prayer:

> The Holy Spirit within us prays to the Father so we can pray according to the will of God. This spirit of prayer, or Spirit-led praying, is the foundation of the corporateness of the prayer meeting. The power of corporate prayer is not in many people praying with each other, but in the uniting of many hearts with the Spirit of God to pray the mind and will of the Father.

The life of the prayer meeting, as well as the direction the meeting takes, is dependent upon the release of the spirit of prayer. There is no great mystery to flowing in the spirit of prayer: one simply allows the Holy Spirit to pray through him. The key to this abandonment to the Spirit is sensitivity. Such sensitivity is cultivated by time spent meditating in God's Word, in worship, and in private prayer.[2]

I believe this understanding will be a great relief to pastors who are discouraged with their corporate prayer meetings. As you teach your congregation to allow the Holy Spirit to pray through them, they will be released into the spirit of prayer. Their prayers will be energized by the Holy Spirit, and revelation will begin to come to pray the burden of the Lord.

It will also help those who "feel dead" or uninspired when they attend a prayer meeting. I've had people say to me, "I want to pray, but I don't know what to say." Others will say, "I come, but I don't 'feel' like praying."

When I hear these comments, I simply respond to people, "Pray in tongues. Allow the Holy Spirit to stir your inner person. Then there will come a liberty and unction to pray both in the Spirit and with the understanding (see 1 Cor. 14:15). You will become sensitive to the burden of the Spirit in that moment."

Understanding the Struggle

Your mind and flesh hate prayer. Your "natural self" wants to be in control and live according to its ideas and opinions. That mindset is the opposite of becoming dependent in prayer on the Holy Spirit. The apostle Paul explained our struggle:

> For the flesh lusteth against the Spirit, and the Spirit against the flesh: and these are contrary the one to the other: so that ye cannot do the things that ye would (Galatians 5:17).

In the moment you were born again, your spirit came alive to God, and you were reconciled to Him; you now have peace with God (see Rom. 5:1). But the Scriptures teach that your soul is being *progressively* saved. That is, your mind must continually be renewed to think God's thoughts and learn His ways (see Rom. 12:1-2; Eph. 4:23).

You must put off the old person, which is "corrupt according to the deceitful lusts" (Eph. 4:22), and put on the new person, which is created in righteousness (see Eph. 4:24). You must learn to speak the truth in love in order to grow up in Christ (see Eph. 4:15). It is the work of the Holy Spirit in your heart that sanctifies you unto a life of holiness.

GETTING HELP

As we learn to yield to the Holy Spirit, He transforms our thinking, changes our desires, and helps us to love God and others. We have a great need to know how the Spirit works in us and through us in prayer. There is no other way to accomplish God's purposes in the earth.

I understand that it is difficult to articulate spiritual truths. Yet through my years of ministry, I have not been shy to ask my mentors to try to express spiritual realities to me that they have experienced. They taught me that it is vitally important to learn to pray in the Spirit daily. When we pray in the Spirit, we are praying directly to our Father, who is Spirit. I embraced the declaration of the apostle Paul, who said he spoke in tongues more than all of his readers (1 Cor. 14:18).

I speak in tongues every day. I do it to build my inner person. I do it to cultivate intimate relationship with my Father. I pray in tongues before I preach the Word to receive a greater anointing. Praying in the Spirit is part of my daily preparation to minister in my spiritual calling.

I have learned that I become more sensitive to the Holy Spirit's correction, to His direction, and to revelation of the Scriptures as I allow Him to pray through me in a divine prayer language. As I yield to the Holy Spirit, His wisdom helps me to confront impossible situations. His love is shed abroad in my heart (see Rom. 5:5), and He fills me with compassion for the hurting and the lost.

Learning to yield to the Holy Spirit in prayer works no matter how you feel. Praying is about making a decision to pray, not about your immediate emotional state regarding prayer. Again, let me recommend to every reader that you pursue the baptism of the Holy Spirit if you have not done so. Jesus said that anyone who asks will receive the Holy Spirit:

> *If ye, then, being evil, know how to give good gifts unto your children: how much more shall your heavenly Father give the Holy Spirit to them that ask him?* (Luke 11:13)

The most delightful thing about yielding to the Holy Spirit is that He continues to teach you about Jesus and to reveal the truths of the Scriptures to your heart. I will never forget, after years of walking in the Spirit, how He opened my understanding to realize that He is much more than a supernatural power in my life. The Holy Spirit is a divine Personality—the Third Person of the Trinity. Once again, my life was forever changed with this wonderful revelation of His personhood.

The battle of prayer is against two things in the earthlies: wandering thoughts, and lack of intimacy with God's character as revealed in His Word. Neither can be cured at once, but they can be cured by discipline.

—Oswald Chambers[1]

CHAPTER 15

THE HOLY SPIRIT IS A DIVINE PERSON

As THE PRAYER REVIVAL CONTINUED, we grew in our understanding of being led by the Holy Spirit into new dimensions of prayer. That first year we prayed as a church several times a week. Because of the saturation presence of the Holy Spirit upon our lives, we became different people. The more we opened our hearts to His convicting power and repented of hidden sin, the more intense His presence became in our prayer meetings and Sunday services.

Before this revival experience, I had known the Holy Spirit as a wonderful, supernatural Presence and Power in my life. He had filled me with the joy of salvation, given me direction for life, and empowered me to pray for others to receive His power. He taught me how to be sensitive to each person and to know how to pray for him or her.

Earlier, I related how the Holy Spirit had touched entire communities to bring salvation, healing, and forgiveness during the first years of my ministry. Yet, in this powerful visitation of the Holy Spirit that our church was experiencing, I began to know the Holy Spirit in a new way.

As He continually softened our hearts and filled us with joy, I watched Him work in many lives in so many different ways. It was during this time I came to know the Holy Spirit as a divine Person.

THE THIRD PERSON OF THE TRINITY

The major characteristics that define personhood are intelligence, will (the ability to choose), and emotions. A person is one who thinks rationally, exercises his or her will, and exhibits a wide spectrum of emotional responses. This personality (our soul), contained in a physical body, is described as our *corporeal* existence.

Of course, we are spiritual beings made in the image of God, who is Spirit (see Gen. 1:26-27). I mentioned earlier that when we are born again, our spirits come alive to God. The Holy Spirit dwells in our spirits, and we become the temple of God (see 1 Cor. 3:16). He wants to govern our soulish lives so that our minds are renewed, our wills submit to the will of God, and our emotions reflect the love of God.

In theological terms, we also describe the Holy Spirit as a Person, the third Person of the Godhead. We are not attributing to Him corporeality; He does not have a physical body, as we have. He is Spirit; He is God. Yet the Scriptures describe the Holy Spirit with attributes of personality. In that way, we are helped in our understanding of how to relate to Him.

For example, Jesus said that the Holy Spirit came to instruct us and to be our Teacher (see John 14:26). The Scriptures declare that no one knows the thoughts of God except the Spirit of God (see 1 Cor. 2:11). The Holy Spirit reveals the mind of God to our spirits. Indeed, He lives within us, continually revealing divine truth to us as we yield to His presence.

The Scriptures describe certain emotional responses of the Holy Spirit as well. They teach us that God is love (see 1 John 4:8). And they declare that the Holy Spirit came to shed the love of God abroad in our hearts (see Rom. 5:5). He came to reveal Jesus to us (see John 16:14), and Jesus came to show us the Father (see John 14:9-10). What a beautiful picture of the Godhead, or Trinity, functioning together as One to make us the people God created us be through redemption.

HURT LOVE

Just as human love can be deeply hurt, so divine love suffers when we sin. The apostle Paul warned believers: "And grieve not the Holy Spirit of God, whereby ye are sealed unto the day of redemption" (Eph. 4:30). Paul shows the kinds of things that grieve the Holy Spirit: corrupt communications, stealing, lying, bitterness, wrath, and evil speaking.

The Scriptures record that the Holy Spirit can be *vexed*, a strong word that means highly displeased, pained. The prophet Isaiah records this sad lament: "But they rebelled, and vexed his Holy Spirit: therefore he was turned to be their enemy, and he fought against them" (Isa. 63:10). The Holy Spirit can be lied to, as Ananias and Sapphira did (see Acts 5). And Peter, preaching to the Jewish people on the day of Pentecost, declared, "...ye do always resist the Holy Ghost..." (Acts 7:51).

Obedience is the opposite of resistance. Our obedience to the commandments of God allows Him to fill us with divine love, peace, joy, and purpose for living. Our disobedience brings negative consequences to our lives and causes grief to the Holy Spirit.

Have you considered that God loves you so much that His emotions are affected by the things you do or fail to do? It follows that, if you want to walk in His presence, you need to avoid all disobedience, which amounts to rebellion.

GETTING TO KNOW HIM

During our prayer revival, most of my waking hours were spent in prayer. Of course, I began my day with devotional prayer. Then, we gathered as leaders to pray for our corporate prayer meetings. I have already described the daily corporate prayer meetings that continued for the first three months of the revival.

As you know, the more time you spend with a person, the better you get to know that person. You see that person in different situations, and you become sensitive to that person's moods. You learn what that person likes and is displeased by. In short, you get to know that person in new ways.

As I spent my days in the presence of the Holy Spirit, I began to see that He expressed different emotions, revealing specific desires for a person or a situation. He made me aware of His purposes for specific situations. He began to guide me in clearer, more intimate ways. I was so aware of His love expressed in His divine personality. This was God manifesting Himself to us and allowing us to know Him in intimate ways.

"Moods" of the Holy Spirit

It is difficult for me to express what an important revelation it was for us to understand that the Holy Spirit desired different "kinds" of prayer according to His divine "mood" or will for the moment. We discovered how to maintain the life of the prayer meeting, its vitality and power, as we learned to please the Holy Spirit and allow Him to pray His will through us.

For example, sometimes when we started a prayer meeting, I could sense that the Holy Spirit was grieved. A "deadness" permeated the entire atmosphere. It restrained the normally spontaneous thanksgiving, petitions, or repentances of the people. I would begin to pray for Him to show us the cause of His grief. Sometimes it was unconfessed sin or personal or corporate disobedience.

As we would open our hearts in prayer, the Holy Spirit would bring true conviction, perhaps to several individuals. They would repent, asking forgiveness for a wrong attitude in their hearts or for ungodly actions. Their heartfelt response to the Holy Spirit's promptings would be followed by a corporate sense of relief and joy that is difficult to explain. We simply experienced a freedom to pray and praise and felt the approval of the Holy Spirit during the rest of the prayer meeting.

As the Scriptures declare, "...Where the spirit of the Lord is, there is liberty" (2 Cor. 3:17). Sometimes, when the "air was cleared," we would begin to sing our praises for His wonderful goodness. On other occasions, a new song would be birthed spontaneously from the exuberant heart of one of our members. We would learn it together and begin to rejoice in this new song that expressed our hearts.

Years later, Dr. Fuchsia Pickett helped us to understand more fully the divine personality of the Holy Spirit. She had been a Methodist professor for years, an avid student of the Word. After a lengthy illness, her prognosis was terminal. Friends invited her to a full gospel church, and she accepted. That morning she was healed and received the baptism of the Holy Spirit.

In her autobiography, *Stones of Remembrance*, she tells how dramatically her life was changed when the Holy Spirit "moved in and became her Teacher":

> The day after I received the baptism of the Holy Spirit, I took a small footstool and sat down as if I were sitting at Jesus' feet. I said these words to my Teacher, the Holy Spirit: "Now, healing has happened to me, and I was taught it was not for today. And I have experienced the baptism of the Holy Spirit in a way that I did not believe in. How do I know that the rest of what I have been taught is right? So let's start over."[2]

In that context, she began her study of the Holy Spirit, verse-by-verse, through the Scriptures (before the computer age of Bible study tools). Years later, she resigned her pastorate in Texas to make her ministry headquarters here at Shekinah. It was then that she began writing her classic trilogy on the Holy Spirit.

How my heart leaped with joy when Dr. Pickett described the moving of the Holy Spirit as we had learned to know Him. She listed seven separate "moods" to the Holy Spirit, which I have paraphrased below:

1. *Conviction* may be defined as an act of pleading, beseeching, or reproving. The Holy Spirit comes to us in this frame of

mind to make us God-conscious and aware of our sinful nature and sinful acts (see John 16:8).

2. *Counseling* mood of the Holy Spirit reveals the divine Teacher. Every new revelation and realm of light we discover in God results from the work of the Holy Spirit, who came to teach us and guide us into all truth (see John 14:26; 16:13).

3. *Compassion* can be called the weeping or tearful mood. It expresses God's tender caring for humankind. Jesus wept over the city of Jerusalem because the Jews missed the day of their visitation (see Luke 19:41-44).

4. *Cleansing* mood of the Holy Spirit was demonstrated in Jesus' zeal to cleanse the temple. As temples of the Holy Spirit (see I Cor. 3:16), this cleansing mood becomes the censoring, holy cry of the inner person. It is the Spirit of God and the spirit of people crying out in union against all that is immoral, sinful, unjust, and destructive to God's kingdom in us.

5. *Commanding* mood of the Holy Spirit was demonstrated when Jesus rebuked the waves and winds and they became calm (see Mark 4:39). It has the authority and power to change any situation for God's glory. It is important to remember, as creatures who love to command, that His commanding mood is motivated by love.

6. *Conquering* mood is the Holy Spirit's expression of triumph, joy, and victory. He confirms the truth: "...For this purpose the Son of God was manifested, that he might destroy the works of the devil" (I John 3:8). Jesus' disciples returned to Him in triumph, saying that "even the devils are subject to us through thy name" (Luke 10:17).

Communion mood of the Holy Spirit, in its broadest sense, encompasses seven different aspects of prayer that the Holy Spirit uses to teach us to communicate with God: petition, thanksgiving, supplication, intercession, praise, worship, and intimate, personal communion of a love relationship with God Himself. Paul prayed for the Corinthians, "The grace of the Lord Jesus Christ, and the love of God, and the communion of the Holy Ghost, be with you all. Amen" (2 Cor. 13:14).[3]

Yielding to the "moods" and desires of the Holy Spirit brought us into a deeper dependency upon Him to make clear the will of God as we were praying together. As we continually waited on the Lord, we learned to identify these "moods" of the Holy Spirit and to cooperate with Him accordingly.

This, of course, was simply a further unfolding of the promise in Romans 8:26-28. He was teaching us to pray according to the will of God. We were astonished at the answers to those prayers and the dimensions of outreach and ministry that were birthed among us as a result.

I am satisfied that if we will just walk in the light of God's Word and make intercession, we can change the lives of our loved ones and the life of our nation.

—Kenneth Hagin[1]

Prayer is therefore not an option for mankind but a necessity. If we don't pray, heaven cannot interfere in earth's affairs. It is imperative that we take responsibility for the earth and determine what happens here by our prayer lives.

—Myles Munroe[2]

CHAPTER 16

BIRTHING GOD'S PURPOSES
THROUGH PRAYER

As we continued our personal and collective journeys into a lifestyle of prayer, our church was beginning to experience weightier, life-changing implications of the challenges of prayer. We would need to become willing to make new commitments of our lives involving our time, energies, and finances to meet them. As we did, we learned that we could not out-give God. The joy and other long-term rewards we received were beyond our wildest dreams as we learned to birth the purposes of God through prayer.

SENSITIVITY TO GOD'S HEART

We began to be more sensitive to God's heart as we felt His burden of love for a person or a specific need in the church. Sometimes we cried out for a particular outreach or ministry God placed in our hearts. At other times, we earnestly entreated God's mercy toward our nation and other nations of the world.

It is fascinating to participate in this kind of burden in corporate prayer. A leader or individual articulates the burden he or she feels from the heart of God. Then others agree with that prayer, sometimes praying a verse of Scripture to add to the cry of the Spirit. The purposes of God become our goal. We desire that these purposes be "birthed" in our lives, in the lives of others, in our communities, in our nation, and beyond.

The Scriptures teach that as we mature in our love relationship with God, He expects us to become fruitful, to bear *much* fruit for the kingdom of God (see John 15). Abiding in Christ through prayer assures that our fruit-bearing is directed by the Spirit of God. It eliminates our "good ideas" for doing things we think will "make a difference."

We began to experience the burden of the Holy Spirit in our corporate prayer meetings so forcefully at times that we understood the "groanings" or yearnings of His heart for a particular situation. Afterward, such peace and joy would flood our hearts that we would spontaneously begin to sing and praise God for the answer, even before we saw it manifest.

And when we did see the answer come, we could scarcely contain our wonder and deep gratitude for having been a part of bringing to birth the purposes of God through prayer. We rejoiced in the fulfillment of the words of Jesus:

> *Ye have not chosen me, but I have chosen you, and ordained you, that ye should go and bring forth fruit, and that your fruit should remain: that whatsoever ye shall ask of the Father in my name, he may give it you* (John 15:16).

NEW DESIRES

Major facets of our ministry that have borne fruit in our church were birthed during those intense times of prayer in that revival. It was fascinating to watch the development of these ministries and their effective results.

As ordinary people, most of our congregation were raising families, earning a living, or getting more education—and serving God. The demands of life were not much different for us than for the average American—except for the unique call of God on our lives to live the reality of Jesus' commandments. That extraordinary desire added a dimension to our lives that would continue to surprise and challenge us.

We continued to expand our conference ministry, sensing the favor of God each time we invited special guest speakers and they accepted our invitation. We were aware that God was strengthening our ministry to pastors as well as enlarging our capacity to serve Him through the truths that were shared.

We also became more involved in missions through the years. We continued our involvement in India and took our youth to Mexico and the Ukraine and to inner city missions in our nation. We have also ministered in Guatemala, Columbia, and Argentina. In turn, the ministers from these nations came to minister to us in the conference ministry at Shekinah.

We can testify that it was the Holy Spirit Himself who put the desire in our hearts for the nations to know Jesus. In our corporate prayer meetings, often someone would read a Scripture about God's love for the nations. Our hearts were melted with desire for them to know Christ.

On different occasions, we experienced the burden of the Holy Spirit to reach the Hindus, Buddhists, Taoists, and other people lost in the worship of false gods. I remember times when we sang a song together that was a prayer for the nations. We would weep with desire for their salvation. Only God could fill our hearts with such love and desire for people we had never seen.

A BIBLE INSTITUTE

As we continued to pray for the nations, God showed us that we should establish a Bible Institute to train people from many nations that He would send to us. One of the inspirational passages that gave impetus to this vision for a training center was the story of Hannah.

She was barren and desired above all else to bear a child. As she prayed desperately, the Scriptures say she made a vow to the Lord:

> And she vowed a vow, and said, O Lord of hosts, if thou wilt indeed look on the affliction of thine handmaid, and remember me, and not forget thine handmaid, but wilt give unto thine handmaid a man child, then I will give him unto the Lord all the days of his life, and there shall no razor come upon his head (I Samuel 1:11).

The Lord answered her prayer and gave her a son, whom she called Samuel. She kept her vow and gave him to serve the Lord in the temple.

OUR FIRST SAMUEL

As the Holy Spirit prayed through us, with weeping and strong desire for the nations, we sought the Lord to let us be fruitful in the harvest of the nations. We asked Him to give us the "Samuels" of His choosing so that we could faithfully train them in the ways of the true God.

We began to prepare faculty and curriculum and facilities for the Bible Institute. It served also as a training school for many of our own congregation. We understood that, as the Holy Spirit gave birth to our cry for salvation among the nations, He would send to Shekinah Bible Institute individuals whom He had called to serve Him in their nations.

It was our part to make a place for them "in the temple." Here we would train them in God's Word, in prayer and worship, and in all the commandments of Jesus we were endeavoring to live. As Hannah made a coat for Samuel, we would be responsible to see that these students were clothed in "garments of salvation" and "the robe of righteousness" (Isa. 61:10).

Amazingly, our first student from the nations was named *Samuel*. He was Samuel Finney, from the well-established Christian network in India in which we were involved. He came with his beautiful wife,

Shulamite, another special Bible name from the Song of Solomon. They trained in our school for three years and returned to India to establish a beautiful church and Bible school.

There they teach the truths of living the commandments of Jesus, developing a prayer lifestyle, and worshiping "in Spirit and truth" as they learned to do while attending Shekinah Bible Institute. Samuel was the first of many students from the nations who graduated from our three-year Bible and theology curriculum.

Many years later, we received a letter from Samuel asking if he and his wife could leave their busy schedule as pastors and leaders in India to return to Shekinah for a season of spiritual refreshing. My purpose in sharing Samuel's story is to show the beauty and power of prayer that brings God's purposes to birth by the Holy Spirit.

There is something very wonderful about the things that are birthed by the Spirit of God. Eternal bonds of relationship are forged with brothers and sisters around the world who share the values placed in their hearts by the Holy Spirit Himself.

Establishing a Bible Institute was not on our "agenda." Yet through prayer we came to understand that it was on God's agenda for us. Thousands of lives have been changed through the ministry of the Bible Institute graduates who returned to their nations to establish schools and churches to reap the harvest.

We were privileged to host students from over a dozen nations, along with many from our nation, on our small campus in Blountville, Tennessee. It is amazing what God will do in answer to the "groanings" of His Spirit in His people.

As the Holy Spirit continued to teach me to pray, He empowered my prayers far beyond the initial, simple petitions I had learned. He led me to pray prayers that He directed, not just prayers for things I wanted. And as our congregation learned to yield to the Holy Spirit in corporate prayer, we rejoiced together at the birth of God's purposes in the nations.

ENJOYING THE "FRUIT" OF OUR LABORS

Recently, on my way to minister in Mozambique, I spent a few days in Johannesburg, South Africa. Reverend Kenneth Meshoe and his wife, Lydia, graduates of our Bible Institute, invited me to their church to teach a worship conference to their large congregation.

Kenneth Meshoe is now very influential in his nation as president of the African Christian Democratic Party (ACDP). He holds a seat in Parliament, while also pastoring a dynamic church of more than three thousand members in Johannesburg.[3] As I observed the impact of their lives and ministry there, I rejoiced in the supernatural reality of "fruit that remains." The Meshoes came to Shekinah Bible Institute as a result of the same kind of "birthing" prayer that brought Samuel Finney from India.

As I prepared to teach their beautiful congregation the truths of biblical worship we had learned, Kenneth introduced me as their mentor in prayer and worship; their words of commendation took my breath away. The divine authority they demonstrated in their persona as well as the love and confidence they exuded were core expressions of their mantle of leadership.

I sat there while they spoke, musing on the sacrifices they made while studying with us: Was this the young couple who came with their babies and willingly lived in a single room in the old farmhouse just so they could experience revival and learn to pray? Could this distinguished, influential couple be the same young students who trudged through the snow to attend the daily prayer meetings, cheerfully and humbly accepting the rigors imposed upon them as with other students?

As I watched them minister with such grace and anointing in the church they had founded, I better understood the words of Paul to his "students":

Therefore, my dear brothers and sisters, stay true to the Lord. I love you and long to see you, dear friends, for you are my joy and the crown I receive for my work (Philippians 4:1 NLT).

I was filled with indescribable joy to know that God had used our church to touch these powerful but humble South African ministers. When we allow the Holy Spirit to pray through us, He brings to birth ministries that are of eternal quality. The enemy will not be able to destroy the results of this eternal fruit; they are what the Scriptures call "fruit that remains" (see John 15:16).

There are other wonderful stories of students from our Bible school who went to the nations to build fruitful ministries where God had given them a vision to establish His kingdom. Some established Bible schools and churches in Indonesia and India. Others raised up churches in Germany and in several nations of Africa.

Some became missionaries to their own cultures, determined to bring truth to overthrow false religions, and some went to other nations as well. Their ministries were birthed as a result of prayer in the power of the Holy Spirit. They were empowered to carry the truth of the gospel through the understanding given them by the Holy Spirit.

During their training at Shekinah Bible Institute, they learned to pray in the power of the Spirit. Of course, learning to pray effectively is a lifetime journey, a lifestyle of learning to yield to the Holy Spirit. Yet the priority of prayer must be established in a life before that can happen.

An Academy for Our Children

The same year that we began to minister to students from the nations in our Bible Institute, the Holy Spirit led us to pray for the destiny of our children. As we prayed, we were impressed to begin a Kindergarten through 12th grade Academy. We felt the Holy Spirit gave us the powerful proverb that warns us to protect children from the wrong kind of education: "Cease, my son, to hear the instruction that causeth to err from the words of knowledge" (Prov. 19:27).

Many children from our church, along with the children of those who came to our Bible Institute, were trained, not only in academics, but also in prayer and developing Christian character. It was heartwarming to see how they responded to the godly atmosphere of their classrooms as they were taught by dedicated Christian teachers. We included our children in our corporate prayer meetings. And they had prayer meetings of their own during their chapel time at school.

There is no greater thrill than to hear the voices of children raised in praise, repentance, and caring prayers for others. Some even received a word of prophecy for the church, an exhortation of what God wanted His people to do or to become. As they were given in childlike honesty, with clarity and simplicity, there was scarcely a dry eye in the congregation when the children finished.

I could give many testimonies of these children who are now raising godly families of their own and making a difference in our community and in the nations of the world.

Provision for "Impossible" Endeavors

You might be wondering how we financed these fruit-bearing endeavors. I am happy that I can honestly say God has done it all through faith in His Word. No, we did not have a benefactor, nor were we a part of a denomination that could fund us. We learned very early the truth of the maxim that where God guides He provides.

In my studies of church history, I had read Hudson Taylor's story about how he financed his mission to China by faith. And I was inspired by godly giants like George Mueller, who trusted God alone to feed his orphans. There were times when there was no food for the day, and Mueller was praying for a miracle. Then he would look up to see food being unloaded to fill his orphans' plates.

Living Sacrificially

Impossible things can be achieved for God when hearts are willing to sacrifice for the establishing of His kingdom. I mentioned the fact that I gave my energies to the ministry for the first seven years without remuneration. I was not the only one who chose to sacrifice personal gain to fulfill the vision of God for our lives.

For example, qualified teachers from our church taught in our K-12 academy without remuneration for many years. They were willing to make this sacrifice to enjoy the fruit of young lives being trained in the ways of God. I will always honor these dedicated teachers for their willingness to do the unusual in order to accomplish the impossible.

We mentioned that a member of one of our founding families, Lowell, Ann's husband, was a contractor. He became the builder for every building project we initiated, working for minimal salary. His "professional" crews consisted of Bible college students and other volunteers from the church. Our church members donated countless hours of building, landscaping, and other work to establish and maintain our God-given vision.

GIVING THE BIBLE WAY

Of course, we taught the biblical principle of tithes and offerings to our congregation, which a large percentage embraced. However, during our prayer revival, some of our church members came to me and said they felt they needed a better understanding of giving. They had read in the Scriptures that it was possible to give a more righteous offering:

> *And he shall sit as a refiner and purifier of silver: and he shall purify the sons of Levi, and purge them as gold and silver, that they may offer unto the Lord an offering in righteousness* (Malachi 3:3).

It may be a little hard to believe that church members would ask the pastor how to please God better in their giving. But remember that we were in revival, and when the Holy Spirit comes in His convicting power, He does things like that.

I began to research the principles of giving in the Scriptures, and I discovered that the Israelites gave three tithes. One was to be used for the Levites (see Num. 18:20-24), one was for the keeping of the sanctuary and sacrifices (see Lev. 27:30-34), and another one was to be given once every three years for the poor (see Deut. 26:12-15).

When I taught these giving principles, the larger part of our congregation began from that time to give according to this pattern. They had a desire to bring their giving to another level to demonstrate their love for God. Because the Holy Spirit had changed our hearts during revival, He made us into a people who loved to give.

Through the years, we have experienced the rewards of sacrificial giving. We have learned how to plant financial seeds expecting a harvest. Our testimony is that the more we give, the more He gives in return. That is simply a biblical principle.

As we would pray about each financial challenge, God would continue to open my understanding as to how He would provide in that situation. This is not to say that there have not been financial struggles. But every time there was a need that greatly stretched our faith, the Holy Spirit would open God's Word and reveal His way of provision.

Visitors who came observed our excellent facilities and learned of the broad outreaches in which we were involved. Often they asked who was underwriting our ministry to enable us to finance all of this. We could only respond that we had no benefactor except the Holy Spirit, working His generosity in the lives of the members of our church. We were learning the truth of Jesus' words that when we seek God first, "all these things shall be added unto you" (Matt. 6:33).

Soon I was to learn another benefit of pursuing a prayer lifestyle. When revival fires burn in your soul, you are able to carry that revival spirit to others. I experienced that personally when I traveled with a team from our church to minister in the beautiful nation of New Zealand.

God shapes the world by prayer. The more prayer there is in the world the better the world will be, the mightier the forces of good against evil.

—E.M. Bounds[1]

CHAPTER 17

SURPRISED BY REVIVAL IN NEW ZEALAND

I N 1985, I WAS INVITED to minister in Christchurch, New Zealand. Some members of pastor Peter Morrow's church had visited our church when we were experiencing our prayer revival. They invited me to come for a week of ministry to teach them about how to enter into revival.

It was exciting to be traveling to another nation where hungry hearts were waiting to learn how to touch God in prayer more effectively. However, I really needed the Holy Spirit to teach me how to pray concerning revival. From my studies of 19th and 20th century revivals, I had learned that true Holy Ghost revival is rare. It had surprised us when we were recipients of His mighty visitation in Blountville, Tennessee.

Yet, I knew that God does respond to hungry hearts that cry to Him for His presence. I read that in the history of our nation, for example, there were several powerful spiritual awakenings that resulted in entire cities and regions being transformed as multitudes of people turned to Jesus (see Appendix D).

GREATER UNDERSTANDING OF REVIVAL

Revival could be described as the saturation presence of God filling a person or a people with His power and love. Because we are made for His presence, when He manifests Himself to us in power, there is a deep desire to commune with Him. Without regard to time, life's distractions fall away, and all we want to do is pray the will of God into being. There is no satisfaction known to people like that of communing spirit-to-Spirit in the presence of God.

At times, He melts your heart so that you weep before Him in wonder and adoration. At other times, He fills you with laughter, praise, and a deep sense of His love and acceptance. Indeed, it is difficult to describe the many aspects of the soul's response to the powerful, manifest presence of its Maker, Redeemer, and Lord.

Leaders who are favored to experience a sovereign spiritual revival, where hearts are truly convicted of sin and lives are transformed, find themselves in largely uncharted waters. The Holy Spirit is the Divine Agent who brings such a revival. He is also the Divine Navigator who must lead us through these uncharted waters.

Revival is much more than religious fervor, special meetings, stirring music, or even personal testimonies. It is the result of life-changing power that emanates from the heart of God through the Holy Spirit touching individuals and entire communities. No human agent, for all their desire to experience such supernatural power, can "teach" people into it or otherwise "make it happen." We were gaining greater understanding of our dependency on Him to bring revival.

I learned that these believers in New Zealand had prayed for many years for a powerful, Holy Ghost-breathed revival. Their fervent prayers were not to go unanswered. When the Holy Spirit anoints people in their prayers for revival, God will hear their cry and give them their hearts' desire.

As it happened, He had another wonderful surprise for us when we arrived in New Zealand. It was exactly the time when God was preparing to send His answer to their prayers for revival.

WHEN GOD'S POWER CAME

Though I still felt I knew little about bringing revival to others, I had learned that prayer is the door opener to revival. Not only is revival a direct result of prayer, but it is also sustained through much prayer. In fact, revival stimulates and deepens desire for earnest, effective prayer.

We had also learned that the powerful, convicting presence of the Holy Spirit is present in revival. It so humbled us that we were eager to confess our faults to one another so that we might be healed. Seeing our sin in His light grieved our hearts and compelled us to turn from it, allowing the blood of Jesus to cleanse us.

As I ministered in a large church in New Zealand, I simply shared some of our experiences from when God came to us in revival. I taught some of the principles of prayer we had learned as a result. After I shared the principles we had learned about prayer and repentance, it was time once again for me to be amazed at the wonderful way God answers prayer.

I watched as the Holy Spirit began to move on the hearts of His people in that large sanctuary in much the same way He had touched the people in our church. From that first meeting, the people began to weep and confess their sins to God and each other. Many went to people to make things right with them. I saw mothers reunited with their grown children, embracing them with tears and repentances. Some people were worshiping and lying prostrate before God; others were crying out to God for forgiveness.

NOTHING TO DO WHEN HE COMES

When the Holy Spirit began to move on the people's hearts, I neither preached nor interfered in any way with what I could see He was doing. Later, the pastor said to me, "I noticed that when God began to move, you did nothing at all from that point."

My answer was one I had learned from our revival experience, "When He is moving, there is nothing else to do." I like to say that revival happens when God gets tired of being misrepresented and shows up to represent Himself.

Julie, one of the ladies who traveled with me, an anointed minstrel, simply sang one hymn after another all evening, acappella. The Holy Spirit did His work among the congregation as they joined her, lifting their voices in song. The simple message of those sacred hymns lifted the congregation ever higher in worship as they expressed their love for the Savior. The truths expressed by those hymn writers seemed electrified in the manifest presence of the Holy Spirit's conviction.

Afterward, I enjoyed listening to some of the cultural expressions of the New Zealanders. I remember one lady who was so thankful for the way God was moving. She exclaimed, jumping up and down, "I'm so glad you came. You blessed my cotton socks off!"

An "Unpredictable" Place

After ministering there, I went directly to a retreat for pastor's wives, where I had been invited to speak. There were 150 women in Christian leadership gathered; they were known as the movers and shakers of the city. All were wives of pastors there.

The retreat was held in a delightful place called Rotorua. It was an area of boiling springs, purported to be rather unstable because of the activity of springs and geysers. An elderly man there said to me, with his unmistakable English accent, "It's an unpredictable place, Rotorua. It's rather like living on a pudding."

In this unusual place, the Holy Spirit moved mightily on those women's hearts. I had learned to keep my heart open in a "pray as you go" posture. These were truly uncharted waters for me. As the presence of the Holy Spirit permeated our hearts, the ladies began to repent before each other. Never mind that these were professionally elite women with considerable standing in their community. Some began to come before the congregation and repent of jealousy and competition regarding their relationships with each other.

Once again, I simply sat and watched as the Holy Spirit was moving on their hearts with His irresistible power of conviction. There is no way to resist the Spirit of Truth. He doesn't come to discuss; He comes to convict. This deep repentance and contrition among these Christian leaders continued for several days. Afterward, I learned of the supernatural joy they received and the contagious power of the Holy Spirit they took back to their churches.

CONFLICTING TRADITIONS

After the retreat, I returned to the church where I had ministered in Christchurch and learned that pastor Peter Morrow had called a meeting of the city's pastors. There were eighty men there who wanted to ask questions about this move of the Holy Spirit. It seems it was beginning to affect most of their churches as a result of what had happened at the Rotorua retreat.

One pastor spoke very seriously to me. He said, "We do not allow women to speak in our church (and I was invited to speak in their largest church). If my wife stands in the church to tell us about what happened in Rotorua, how can we enter in? We will be violating our policy on the place of women in the church."

Then, quite sincerely, he added, "Please understand, we do want revival like the women have experienced it. And at present, we have no revival in our church." He simply did not know how to handle this conundrum of the Holy Spirit moving among the women.

I listened quietly and prayerfully. His dilemma brought to mind "doctrinal" issues that I had to resolve as a woman called into ministry. As I listened, the Holy Spirit showed me how to answer this man. Kindly, I said, "Your wife seems to be the designated torchbearer for your church. Through her experience in this revival, she has received an anointing to introduce your church to real Holy Ghost revival."

Then, to the group of ministers seated there, I offered, "Didn't God know when He visited your wives at Rotorua that you pastors would have to deal with this policy question? It seems to me now that you have to make a choice: between experiencing the revival you desire or hold-ing to your teaching regarding women's participation in the church."

Months after I had returned to Tennessee, I learned from my friends in New Zealand that the pastors' wives did indeed give their testimonies in their own churches. As a result, "little revivals" sprang up around the city.

The Holy Spirit is faithful to move everywhere people are hungry for God's presence and receptive to hear what He will do. When He is allowed to move in His own powerful way, unhindered by human efforts, traditions, and opinions, He will guide us into all truth and bless us with His divine presence.

My lifelong pursuit of the presence of God had taken me to won-derful places and had brought godly men and women into our lives as a church. It had opened avenues of ministry at home and abroad that were beyond my wildest imaginings. But it seemed the Holy Spirit was just getting started, after all these years, in giving me my heart's desire—to be a part of what He is doing in the earth.

Oh brother, pray; in spite of Satan, pray; spend hours in prayer; rather neglect friends than not pray; rather fast and lose breakfast, dinner, tea, and supper—and sleep too—than not pray. And we must not talk about prayer, we must pray in right earnest. The Lord is near.

—Andrew A. Bonar[1]

CHAPTER 18

SEEKING HIS PRESENCE—ANYWHERE

"LORD," I HAD PRAYED FERVENTLY, "I just want to be where You are moving in the earth. No place is too far for me to go; nothing is too hard for me to do. I am no longer in charge of my life or my time. Just let me be a part of what you are doing in the earth: anything, anywhere, anytime, anyway." My insatiable desire to experience the moving of His Spirit had motivated me to make that unconditional promise to God.

I understood what every student of the Scriptures knows, that God is omnipresent. That is, He is present everywhere all the time. And born-again Christians know that the Holy Spirit dwells within them, as the apostle Paul affirms: "Know ye not that ye are the temple of God, and that the Spirit of God dwelleth in you?" (I Cor. 3:16).

Still, the Scriptures in both Old and New Testaments exhort us to seek God with our whole hearts, promising that we will find Him (see Deut. 4:29; Matt. 6:33). Here is another divine paradox: God is everywhere, yet we must seek Him to find Him. Our failure to understand this paradox sometimes keeps us from knowing God as we desire to know Him.

Too many times our natural minds think in terms of "either/or" instead of "both/and." Though God is everywhere, and though I know He dwells in my heart by faith, I can never stop seeking Him with my whole heart if I am to know Him in His fullness. The Holy Spirit has brought me into more powerful realms of prayer through this determination to seek His presence wherever He is moving.

AWAKENING TO THE "NOW" REVIVAL

Some believers and even pastors do not understand the significance of opening their eyes and hearts to what God is doing in other "streams of ministry" in other parts of the world. Instead, they are preoccupied with the latest financial problem of their church, the next building project, their own career change, or other "local" involvements. Living within these narrow parameters, they miss the opportunity to learn and grow; they are oblivious to what God is doing at any given time in the earth.

Are you aware that entire African nations, once steeped entirely in voodoo and witchcraft religions, now consider themselves to be Christian nations and are governed by Christian presidents? Leaders seek counsel from godly prophetic ministries in their nations before making important decisions that affect their people.

Do you know that people are being raised from the dead in Africa in Jesus name according to the biblical injunction of Christ to His disciples: "Heal the sick, cleanse the lepers, raise the dead, cast out devils: freely ye have received, freely give" (Matt. 10:8). These signs are following believers in many other countries.

Seeking to find God *anywhere* He is moving in power has been a part of my *modus operandi* throughout four decades of ministry. I am a student of the Holy Spirit; He is my Teacher. I will always seek to learn His ways wherever He is moving in the lives of people supernaturally.

Witnessing revival where God is moving raises our awareness of God's great desire to transform lives, communities, and entire nations. It strengthens our faith and expectation for what God will do when we determine to seek Him with all our hearts. We can be a part of what

He is doing if we will open our spiritual eyes and ears and seek His presence.

It is a fact that God manifests His power and presence in different places at different times—for His reasons. That is why I continually ask Him to allow me to be a part of what He is currently doing. I have learned that there will be concentrated moves of His Spirit in which He visits His people and gives them revelation of what His purposes are for that specific season.

Always, when there is a special outpouring of the Holy Spirit, you can trace that powerful visitation to a people who have been praying fervently for revival. When God manifests His presence in answer to those prayers, He brings physical, emotional, and spiritual healing, salvation, and restoration to many people. Communities and entire nations are transformed as a result of answered prayer.

THE HARVEST IN THE UKRAINE

I shared earlier that I first traveled to the former communist bastion of the Ukraine in 1994, where the Bible had been banned for seventy years. After ten days of ministry, the youth team we brought had given out over three thousand Bibles. We did not announce that we had Bibles; we only gave them to those who responded to an invitation to accept Jesus as their Savior.

We were thrilled to be a part of such a wonderful harvest. For two years following, we produced television programs of our services that aired on Ukrainian television, reaching many for Christ. And we continued to travel to the Ukraine for several years.

On one of those subsequent trips, I was told that the milkmaids who worked for a dairyman had become aware of our ministry in the area. They asked if I would come and tell them about Jesus. I agreed, and we were taken to a large dairy barn. Some chairs were arranged in a circle in the middle of the barn. (Our first services at Shekinah were conducted in an old barn, but this one was still fully functional.)

I looked around, and it seemed that my audience was going to be both milkmaids and the men who worked to keep the barn shoveled and clean. Through an interpreter, I began to present the simple gospel message, but one of the men stood up and interrupted my message, yelling in frustration.

Startled, I asked my interpreter what was happening. "He's very agitated," the interpreter answered. "He wants to know just exactly who Jesus is. He says that you are not telling him about Jesus."

In that unsettling uproar, the Holy Spirit came to my rescue. I said, "You know, Jesus is the Son of God. He came to this earth by being birthed through a woman, so He knows all about how we think and feel. He was so humble that He was born in a place just like this—among cattle and hay. He is the King of the universe, but He wasn't born like a king. He was born like the people He loved enough to die for. That would be you, sir, and me. Don't you want to receive Him as your Savior?"

I learned later that some people from false cults had been teaching in the area. These dairy workers were afraid they would be deceived. They wanted to know about the real God. So this man came straight to the point. He cried out, "Just tell me about Jesus." What a privilege! The Holy Spirit will always respond to such hungry hearts who want to know the truth.

On a later trip to the Ukraine, I witnessed strong Christian churches that have been established in just a few years. Many ministers have gone to the Ukraine and stayed to reap the harvest. Besides winning thousands of souls to Jesus, the social and educational programs of these churches are so effective that the Ukrainian government is supporting many of them financially and promoting them throughout the nation.[2]

They are part of the "Now Revival" of what God is doing. In my search to see God moving *anywhere*, I have visited with strong Christian leaders in the Bahamas, Columbia, Argentina, Guatemala, India, and several nations in Africa. In their churches, I have experienced firsthand the exuberance of thousands of godly Christians who have been redeemed from atheism, voodoo, witchcraft, and other godless philosophies.

I have participated in all-night prayer meetings in Africa where thousands of people pray fervently throughout the night. During their praise and worship, miracles of healing begin to happen and lost souls receive Jesus as Savior. I have preached in Colombia, South America, in a church where thousands come to pray every day. In many nations, the central focus of Christians' lives is seeking God in prayer.

As I have witnessed the "Now Revival," my resolve has been strengthened to press into new dimensions of prevailing prayer. Believers in these nations cannot settle for "church as usual" during one hour on Sunday. They have to seek the true God and Savior, Jesus Christ. They need the power of the Holy Spirit to see His supernatural power break the strongholds of false religions, witch doctors, and so forth.

UNEXPECTED IMPARTATION

After ministering in the Ukraine in 1994, I heard of a powerful visitation of God's Spirit in another nation that same year. In my zeal to know where God is moving, I do not pursue any specific "rumor" before I check it out with mentors and other credible leaders. Satisfied that God was truly doing wonderful things there, my husband and I quietly made a trip to see firsthand what God was doing. I did not publicize my going in order to not raise expectations of my congregation prematurely.

Through my experience of the visitations of God in other nations where I visited or led revivals, I had learned that there is a reality of impartation as the Scriptures reveal. People can receive a greater anointing of the Holy Spirit through the laying on of hands.

The apostles taught the principle of the laying on of hands to receive the baptism of the Holy Spirit (see Acts 8:18). And Paul referred to the impartation of spiritual gifts to Timothy through the laying on of hands (see 1 Tim. 4:14). The writer to the Hebrews also mentions the doctrine of the laying on of hands as a basic principle of the doctrine of Christ (see Heb. 6:1-2).

When my husband and I arrived at the place of the meeting, we were immediately aware of a powerful presence of the Holy Spirit touching lives. Assured that God was doing a wonderful thing in that place, I asked the leaders to pray for me. I was open to receiving the laying on of hands from godly leaders once I experienced the genuineness of God's presence there.

As they laid hands on me, because of the power of the anointing, I fell to the floor. I was unable to stand in this awesome presence of God. I recalled this biblical phenomenon from instances when God manifested His powerful presence to a person (see Dan. 8:18; John 18:6; Rev. 1:17).

Words cannot describe the overwhelming peace, love, and joy that I felt as I lay there for about half an hour. As I was weeping quietly, God's love engulfed my mind and spirit and erased any earthly concerns or cares. There was no sense of "impropriety" that would make me self-conscious about lying there. I felt bathed in His love and utterly secure in His manifest presence with me.

Afterward, I was not aware that anything dramatic or life-changing had happened to me. But the next day, as we were returning home, I realized that I had received a miraculous healing in the emotional realm. I had been deeply hurt by a difficult relational problem years earlier. Any thought of it would fill me with pain.

There is no pain like that which results from a broken friendship or lost family relationship. The memories are too many and too deep to "just forget." It breaks the mind and cripples the emotions. Forgiveness of the "offense" alone does not take the grief. Only Jesus has the answer to that kind of grief.

That is why He came—to heal the brokenhearted (see Luke 4:18). Only He can heal in such a way that will impart to us His peace that passes understanding (see Phil. 4:7). When you have lived with emotional pain for an extended time, it becomes part of your psyche, a kind of unwelcome "companion" of misery.

On our way home, I became aware that my terrible "companion" was no longer there. My deliverance had been instantaneous and super-natural. Jesus had healed me from a terrible, seemingly incurable wound that had happened years earlier. Just one touch of God's power through the anointed hands of His servants had brought me supernatural heal-ing and release from emotional pain.

I was free! I felt like I could live again! Whenever God draws near in a move of the Spirit, which we call "revival" or "outpouring," He heals every aspect of our beings. That is because His name is Healer (Jehovah-Rapha).

A NEW ANOINTING

What I did not know was that, beyond my own healing, I had received the same wonderful, healing anointing that the Holy Spirit would impart to others through prayer and the laying on of hands. I did not know that, as I yielded to that anointing, the Holy Spirit would take our congregation, as well as other churches where I ministered, into a new dimension of His healing power for body, soul, and spirit.

Those who worked in leadership with me would also receive this impartation and minister with me in this healing anointing. Later, I learned that other churches across the nation were also experiencing this same outpouring of the Holy Spirit.

The following Sunday morning, after I ministered the Word, some people responded to a call to come forward for prayer. I still had not made my congregation aware of my visit to those revival meetings. They did not know about my experience of emotional healing in the presence of the Holy Spirit a few days earlier. They merely wanted me to pray for them in response to the message I had preached, perhaps for an anger problem or some other personal need.

As I laid hands on them and prayed for each person, I saw again the promise of the Scripture fulfilled to do exceeding abundantly above what we are able to ask or think (see Eph. 3:20). No one in our congregation would have asked for what the Holy Spirit did that morning. Few had even seen it before; most did not know that it could happen.

"JUST GET OUT OF THE WAY"—AGAIN

When I simply raised my arm and extended it over the head of a lady who stood in the line for prayer, not actually touching her, I literally felt a wind blow from behind me. It blew through my hair and rearranged it. And it "blew" the woman standing there to the floor. I recalled that on the day of Pentecost a sound of a rushing mighty wind occurred when the Holy Spirit was first poured out in the upper room (see Acts 2).

I looked on in astonishment as a lady at the other end of the line to my left also "blew over." A doctor standing behind her tried to catch her fall, but the same "wind" blew him over. Soon most of the people standing in front of me were lying on the floor, lost in their own experience with God. I never touched any of them, never even prayed for them.

Wait a minute, Holy Spirit, you're working before I can pray, I thought.

I sensed His response: "You've already prayed and asked to be in the middle of what I am doing. I am answering your prayer. All you have to do is get out of the way. I have given you an anointing to give to needy people; it is an anointing for healing that will set them free. I will teach you how to lead by following my Leadership."

When I turned to walk away from that line of people now lying on the floor, I felt a sensation like electricity in my feet and legs. Then I felt it strongly in my hands. From that time forward, when the Holy Spirit's anointing was there to heal, I would feel that sensation in my hands.

As I walked around the sanctuary to pray for others who had lingered to observe all that was happening, they had similar experiences to those who came forward for prayer. They were unable to stand in that place of the anointing of the Holy Spirit. Later, we would hear wonderful testimonies of what the Holy Spirit did for them as they lay there on the floor in His powerful presence.

My Divine Teacher Is so Faithful

The Holy Spirit instructed me further, "As you keep your appointment to worship the Father every morning, I will help you to love Him more deeply. You will begin to see Jesus more clearly and experience His compassion for people who need so desperately to be delivered and set free. This intimate relationship with the Father will cause you to be moved by an overwhelming compassion to reach out to people in His name."

I acknowledged then that, without the Holy Spirit doing a work in my heart, I couldn't possibly have the compassion of God I needed for this ministry. That fact would become exceedingly clear in the coming months, when I sometimes ministered to hundreds of people for hours at a time. Once again, I was walking in a new measure of dependence on the Holy Spirit.

I began to get the picture. I had learned from the beginning that I was to do my praying in advance. From that prayer posture, as I walked in this new anointing, I only had to lay my hands on them in faith. God would do what He wanted to do in their lives.

He explained to me the sensation I felt in my hands when His anointing was there:

> When you begin to testify to what I have done for you, you will feel electricity in the palms of your hands. That is when you should pray for the people. The more strongly you feel it, the greater will be the level of anointing that will flow when you pray for people. Remember, this is not your

anointing; it is Mine. It is not your ministry; it is Mine. You will not need to know for whom, how, or when to pray in your own intellect. You are only to be a yielded vessel; the power is Mine.

DIVINE SURGERY ERADICATED HATRED

Sometimes we become enamored by physical manifestations of the presence of God. But the greatest thing we experienced during this fresh visitation of the Holy Spirit was that the brokenhearted were healed. Captives were delivered, the bruised were set at liberty, and salvation was preached to the poor just as Jesus promised (see Luke 4:18).

One testimony that stands out in my memory came from a visitor to our church. He shared with us that when the opportunity was given to receive prayer, he came forward. In that moment, he was not considering his conflict with his business partner. He confessed that when he came to church, he was consumed with a desire to murder this man, who had cheated him out of his share of their business.

Yet, when he received prayer, the anointing of the Holy Spirit touched him, and he too fell to the floor. He said, "When I finally struggled up from the floor in somewhat of a stupor, I went to sit in my chair. But I felt as if I had left something on the floor. Something was missing. My billfold? No, it was in my pocket. My Bible? It was beside me on the chair."

Through his laughter and tears, he finally managed to say, "What was missing was the ball of hatred that had been in my chest since my partner betrayed me. It's gone. I'm free." Then, with a sense of incredible wonder, he repeated again and again, "I'm free! I'm free!" Weeping with him, I could relate to his deliverance from his "unwelcome companion."

He was a nice Methodist guy who never expected to experience such a supernatural touch of the Holy Spirit. He said to me privately, "When you laid your hands lightly on my head, I felt like your finger became a knife that went down into my skull, cutting away the hatred in my mind."

There were many such testimonies of dramatic life changes during that powerful time of visitation. The Holy Spirit was continually teaching me how to pray for people in this powerful and unexpected outpouring of revival. Most of the time, I did not know the people for whom I was praying. I did not pray specific words "with knowledge" because I had no idea what kind of deep spiritual and emotional needs the people might have.

I simply called on the Holy Spirit, and He did His supernatural work as I laid my hands in faith on those who came for prayer. I had done my praying in secret; the Holy Spirit was doing His work in public.

In the year following, every time I ministered in our sanctuary or elsewhere when I traveled in ministry, these marvelous manifestations of the Holy Spirit would occur—all because I had simply "heard" of a powerful outpouring of the Holy Spirit in another country and went with my husband to "check it out." Because I was willing for "anything, anywhere, anytime, anyway" that would bring me into the redeeming presence of God.

When I traveled to the Ukraine again, they referred to the phenomenon of falling under the anointing of the Holy Spirit as, "this miraculous blessing." In Jamaica, I saw something I had never seen before. When I prayed for people, they would fall to the floor with no one there to help break their fall. (In our sanctuary, we provided ushers who would stand behind and lower people gently to the floor.) For the Jamaicans, the Holy Spirit provided a "cushion."

I can say this because I saw it myself. It was as if an invisible pillow was placed under each person before they connected abruptly with the floor. No one was ever harmed, no matter their physical condition. More importantly, they met God and received the answer to their personal needs.

HEAVENLY VISIONS AND POWERFUL DELIVERANCE

In a family camp where I minister every summer, we experienced the same powerful moving of the Holy Spirit. It is an awesome sight to see entire congregations lying on the floor. They are lying in the presence of God rejoicing and weeping, their lives obviously being touched powerfully by the Holy Spirit working in their souls. Afterward, many gave testimony of the tangible changes God had made in their lives.

Small children cannot be expected to lie still for any length of time unless they are asleep. Yet, when they were prayed for and experienced this anointing of the Holy Spirit, some lay on the floor for hours. In their candid, child's vocabulary, some shared the wonders they had seen during their visit to heaven as they lay on the floor.

Very special in my memory is the experience of a sixteen-year-old girl who was "under the power of the Spirit" for such an extended time that I became concerned. Her friends moved their sleeping bags into the chapel and spent the night with her there. At nine o'clock the next morning, she finally came out of the "trance" she had experienced that lasted for hours.

I went to the chapel early that morning to check on her. I had not yet witnessed a visitation this intense in someone's life. I was relieved when she rallied, and I wanted to know if she was alright. I asked her gently, "Where did you go last night?"

She replied, "Oh it was so wonderful. I was with Jesus the whole time. And now I know He loves me, and He will be my reason for living."

I later learned what others already knew. Her father had abused her. Her mother was involved in witchcraft. Life was such a burden that this young girl wasn't sure she wanted to live at all. I wept for joy at her deliverance, at the unspeakable kindness of Jesus to heal this precious young life from the treachery that had scarred her soul. This is real freedom, being set at liberty from your bruises that no one else sees.

Jesus died for this. Thank God, through the anointing of the Holy Spirit, He allows us to be a part of His ministry to desperate and needy people.

What the church needs today is not more machinery or better, not new organizations or more novel methods, but men whom the Holy Ghost can use—men of prayer, men mighty in prayer.

—E.M. Bounds[1]

We have to pray with our eyes on God, not on the difficulties.

—Oswald Chambers[2]

CHAPTER 19

LEARNING TO PRAY STRATEGICALLY

URING THE LAST FIFTEEN YEARS, my search for the moving of the Holy Spirit in the earth has continued. It has led me to a deepening of my devotional prayer life. And it has taken me to other nations and brought more godly Christians into my life. Our church continues to cultivate a prayer lifestyle as we seek to fulfill our destiny of establishing His kingdom.

It is important to be sensitive to the ebb and flow of the moving of God. His visitations do not continue indefinitely. Some who have tried to "continue" in the way they have grown comfortable with God moving, when His anointing is no longer there, have gone astray. When God moved us sovereignly into a prayer revival for three months, His presence was so strong that we could do nothing but pray. But there came an ebb to the intensity of that visitation, and we had to learn to adjust our lives accordingly.

Yet God is always hearing and answering prayer. And He is working to establish His kingdom through obedient hearts. I am still seeking to pray more effectively and with greater authority, to see signs and wonders, and to fulfill the purposes of God. We must ever be learning to hear the voice of the Lord for His battle plans against the enemy.

I was told that on one occasion, when Hezbollah fired over 800 missiles into Israel, only fifty hit their mark to inflict damage. That means that 750 missiles failed in their attempt to bring strategic results against their enemy. I thought immediately how that ineffectiveness relates to our praying at times.

When we pray "buckshot prayers" that are not really aimed at anything, sure enough, we don't inflict damage on the enemy or gain access to the kingdom of God. General and unspecific prayers to "bless the pastor" and "help the poor" and "watch over those in danger" are not very powerful.

Continuing the war metaphor, let's contrast Hezbollah's ineffectiveness with our U.S. forces' strategic precision during the Gulf War. Targeting the enemy, from high above the earth, aircraft weapons were able to pinpoint specific buildings or underground bunkers where the enemy lurked, taking them out without causing damage to innocent civilians.

Surely, when we search the Scriptures, we can attest to this same kind of strategic precision in the prayers recorded there. The requests of God's people were specific; they were based on the promises of God that had been revealed to them. And in both Old and New Testaments, the answers they sought are recorded for all to know.

STOP THIS WESTERN PRAYING

Several years ago, as I traveled to the nations of Africa where God was moving miraculously, I observed a more powerful approach to prayer that I wanted to make a part of my life. I was introduced to ministers who had broken through dark bondages of the occult and witchcraft that had oppressed people for hundreds of years.

Through their ministries, based entirely in prayer and faith in God's miraculous power, multitudes of people were saved and set free from their deceptions, choosing to serve Jesus. Many testified to miraculous healings, some to being raised from the dead. I saw huge churches of joyful, zealous Christians making prayer a lifestyle and reaping the rewards of the abundant life God promised us.

I realized that this kind of vibrant Christianity that overcomes blatant powers of the devil requires greater power in prayer than we were experiencing. I began to ask the Holy Spirit to teach me to pray strategically and to empower me to implement it in our church.

As a result of my experience during several years, I discovered dynamic principles of prayer employed by my African friends. It was so life-changing that it inspired me to write the book, *Prayer in Another Dimension.*[3] Once again, my search for God's presence had been rewarded by the faith to believe Him for greater power in prayer.

On one of my visits to Africa, I was a guest of the church of Bishop Duncan-Williams in Ghana. He is considered the father of the charismatic movement in Ghana. The president of Ghana looks to him as one of his chief advisors. His influence extends to other African nations and to many hundreds of churches. That was not always the case.

Duncan-Williams' father was a spiritist who worked effective curses and was involved in occult practices. Yet his son, Nicholas, desperately sought for the true God to deliver him from his own self-destructions. He wanted to be free from carrying on the spiritist tradition of his family. His story is worth telling, but with little space here, let me give you the conclusion of the matter.

Duncan-Williams was redeemed from the satanic curses on his life and from sin. And God has used him to build churches in his country and mentor countless youth to become strong Christian leaders as well. His church, built on his knees, numbered 12,000 at that time. Archbishop Duncan-Williams is known in many parts of the world as the Apostle of Strategic Prayer.[4]

When I visited Ghana, I participated in their weekly Jericho prayer meeting that regularly drew four thousand people. They prayed fervently, standing on their feet for three hours. Leaders exhorted them to pray the Word of God. Some shouted, some walked, and some clapped their hands. In summary, they kept a powerful focus on the business of heaven in which they were engaged for the entire time of prayer.

I heard Duncan-Williams, who ministers to many churches in our nation, speak these radical words to an American congregation: "Stop this Western praying!" He continued, "These nice prayers are not getting you anywhere. You've got to get mad at the devil! You have to enforce the Word of God against his deceptive destructions."

As I listened intently, I understood that the "Western praying" to which Duncan-Williams referred is an insipid, faithless, praying that lacks in authority and focus. Even sincere believers are sometimes caught in this kind of praying. This lack of faith ultimately reflects a lack of desire to see the kingdom of God come and the will of God be done "on earth as it is in heaven."

PRINCIPLES OF STRATEGIC PRAYING

I have discussed in earlier chapters the principles of prayer on which we had founded our ministry and the miracles that resulted. We were desirous to be about the Father's business and to make His house a house of prayer for all nations. Yet I was keenly aware, as I listened to these African pastors, that I was being introduced to a new level of authority in prayer. It involved an intensity, focus, perseverance, and greater revelation of the supernatural power of prayer that brings results of "biblical proportions."

These African leaders understand the divine imperative of wrestling "against principalities, against powers, against the rulers of the darkness of this age, against spiritual hosts of wickedness in the heavenly places" (Eph. 6:12 NKJV). They have learned to contend for the promises of God to His children in order to live the abundant life—in every aspect of life.

They live focused lives as the Scriptures teach, spending much time in the Word and in prayer. They have released the power of God to such an extent that they are seeing their entire nations coming to Jesus. Christians are holding prominent positions in government and in the schools, hospitals, and other "marketplaces" of their culture.

They are eradicating poverty, disease, voodoo, and other satanic practices. Because they understand the power of the spirit world from the dark side, they are intent on doing it damage through the power of Jesus' name.

This dimension of prayer focuses on recognizing the defeat of the devil, which Jesus accomplished on the cross. Placing our faith in that finished work of Calvary, the Africans teach us to insist on the enemy's immediate release of every good thing that God has promised to His children.

ADOPTING A BIBLICAL PRAYER LIFESTYLE

In these nations where I have visited and observed God moving mightily, I have learned that it is normal for believers to be continually involved in prayer as a lifestyle, both corporately and individually. You can go to their sanctuaries at any hour of the day or night and find believers praying, intensely, earnestly. Their churches have truly become what Jesus ordained them to become: "a house of prayer for all nations."

The Holy Spirit impressed upon me that, as American Christians, we desperately need a paradigm shift concerning our commitment to prayer. If we believe the words of Jesus, that the church's biblical purpose is to become a house of prayer, we will have to pray more than a few minutes a day. We will have to commit our lives to becoming men and women of prayer.

Throughout history, prayer has played a much bigger part in cultures than it does today. The nation of Israel was accustomed to praying three times a day as their regular lifestyle. The Scriptures record that Daniel prayed three times a day (see Dan. 6:10). The psalmist David declared, "Evening, and morning, and at noon, will I pray, and cry aloud: and he shall hear my voice" (Ps. 55:17).

In the Scriptures, we read phrases like, "...his praise shall continually be in my mouth" (Ps. 34:1) and "...to do sacrifice continually"

(Jer. 33:18). When David established the tabernacle, he set people in place to worship and praise and call on God 24/7.

In the book of Acts, we read of the early church keeping the hours of prayer and praying all night. In the Jewish culture today, devout Jews still pray three times a day. And in India, I witnessed the cultural phenomenon of Muslims responding to a call to prayer five times a day.

The prayer lives of Christians in these "revival nations" closely resemble the fervency of the Old Testament prophets as well as the New Testament Church. I believe that when we learn to yield our hearts and minds to these biblical patterns of prayer, we will begin to see the power of God released in our churches, our communities, and our nation. It is time for American churches to take a quantum leap into prayer in another dimension.

We must grasp the fact that the *essence* of true prayer is *spiritual* rather than intellectual. It must be accomplished through the Holy Spirit working effectively through our relationship with God. In other words, we have to cultivate more intimate relationship with Jesus to have greater results in prayer.

We have to lay aside prayers based only on logic and our knowledge. Analyzing situations and explaining them to God is a futile attempt at effective prayer. God's perspective of life is very different from ours. Only in touching His heart for a person or situation, or our own destiny, can we begin to see supernatural results. This is the powerful prayer that Christians are experiencing in other nations.

ELEMENTS OF STRATEGIC PRAYER

My friend, Pastor Bart Pierce of Baltimore, traveled to these African nations to observe revival as I did. When he ministered in our church, he shared some key elements he had distilled from the effective praying he observed there:

1. Their prayers are *vocal*, rather than silent or quiet.

2. They pray *fervently*, focused on specific needs.

3. They consistently pray the Word in faith—*through proclamation.*

4. Their entire focus is *vertical,* addressing God alone.

Their prayers are full of the authority of *prophetic* anointing.[5]

I began to study the biblical foundation for each of these characteristics of revival praying. As I did, it became very clear to me, by contrast, the lack of fervency, focus, authority, and prophetic anointing that characterizes much of the praying in our American churches. We can learn from others who are experiencing the supernatural presence of God with miracles and signs following. It is time we embrace the biblical pattern of prayer they have made a lifestyle.

MAKE PRAYER VOCAL

I cried unto the Lord with my voice, and he heard me out of his holy hill. Selah (Psalm 3:4).

I am convinced that one of the greatest weaknesses we have in prayer is a sense of intimidation or ignorance about being vocal in our prayers. Perhaps it is because we have not developed a prayer vocabulary. Have you ever said, "I want to pray, but I don't know what to say"?

In the Holy Ghost-breathed revivals, I have observed that when the Holy Spirit breaks in upon a people, they begin to speak, pray, sing, and cry to the Lord freely. It becomes easy to repent, to exhort, to prophesy, to testify—all verbal expressions that may have seemed out of character for some. But when God stirred their hearts in His manifest presence, it was "natural."

You have in your grasp a powerful tool against the enemy when you learn to speak the Word of God boldly in prayer. The devil does not want you to know the tremendous victories you will experience when you begin to pray the promises of God's Word. We have prayed our fears, our unbelief, our confusion, and our opinions. None of these prayers are powerful against the enemy.

Instead, I encourage you to begin to praise God with all your strength and lift your voice to petition God's purposes. Open the book of Psalms and pray aloud the prayers of David that fit your situation and heart cry. When you pray the Word of God, you are praying the answer, not the problem. It is a direct route to the unadulterated will of God.

I am not saying that you should never tell God your thoughts or voice your questions. You should have conversations with God, both devotionally and in presenting your petitions. But you have developed a habit of weak praying when you do not pray the divinely-inspired promises of God.

PRAY FERVENTLY WITH PERSEVERANCE

I wrote earlier about receiving power to bring to birth the purposes of God for Shekinah. I later heard Bishop Duncan-Williams explain: *"Prayer is the womb that births the promises and prophecies of God."*

When we consider this analogy of prayer as a womb, we can relate to the pressure, pain, and perseverance needed to bring the answer to "birth." The Word of God is the seed deposited in the womb of prayer. In that place of prayer, the Holy Spirit nurtures the seed until it comes to fullness of time and maturity, ready to be birthed. We understand, then, that the answer to prayer is made manifest through the working of the Holy Spirit.

Regarding perseverance in prayer, Bishop Duncan-Williams encourages believers to make a lifetime commitment to birthing the promises and prophecies of God in prayer.

Make prayer a lifestyle. Commit to it until you die. The reason we don't have miracles in the church today is that we don't pray. Take it up another level. Apply more pressure to the enemy. *Make up your mind to "push" to birth the purposes of God.* When you feel the pain of travail, don't stop praying.[6]

MAKE PROCLAMATIONS IN PRAYER

The Holy Spirit gives us an unction, or anointing, to declare God's truth in prayer:

> *But ye have an unction from the Holy One, and ye know all things…but the anointing which ye have received of him abideth in you, and ye need not that any man teach you: but as the same anointing teacheth you of all things, and is truth, and is no lie, and even as it hath taught you, ye shall abide in him* (I John 2:20,27).

According to *Vine's Expository Dictionary of New Testament Words*:

> Having an unction from the Holy One means believers have an anointing that renders them holy, separating them to God. This passage teaches that the gift of the Holy Spirit is the all-efficient means of enabling believers to possess a knowledge of the truth.[7]

He gives us the burden of God's heart and shows us the will of God in prayer. As I have said, the Holy Spirit Himself prays the will of God through us when we do not know how to pray as we should (see Rom. 8:26). He helps us to make the proclamation of Scriptures that contain divine promises become the will of God for our lives and situations. I explained in my book, *Prayer in Another Dimension*:

> Satan wants to keep God's people from making biblical declarations. He hates it when we say: "I am the righteousness of God in Christ"; "I am the healed of the Lord"; "I am blessed and highly favored." The devil trembles when we make biblical proclamations:
>
> *Now thanks be to God who always leads us in triumph in Christ* (2 Corinthians 2:14 NKJV).
>
> *For by You I can run against a troop, by my God I can leap over a wall* (Psalm 18:29 NKJV).

Oh, sing to the Lord a new song! For He has done marvelous things; His right hand and His holy arm have gained Him the victory (Psalm 98:1 NKJV).[8]

KEEP YOUR FOCUS *VERTICAL*

When I participated in African prayer summits, I observed that they not only prayed with focused intensity and great fervency, but that their entire concentration was on God alone. That is striking, considering the thousands of people there who could have engaged in "spectatorship," private conversations, and so forth. Instead, every person I witnessed was praying aloud in agreement with one person who led in prayer for specific needs.

These precious believers had learned how to pray the Scriptures, how to make declarations and proclamations of the promises of God, pouring them out to God for the supernatural answers they needed. It is not surprising that in this atmosphere of dynamic spiritual energy, miracles and healings began to happen to the people present.

There is such a freedom among these praying Christians—freedom from the fear of people's faces, the opinions of others, and "doing it wrong." Their single-eyed focus on God alone reflects the desire they have to receive supernatural answers to their prayers. They understand that they are praying for spiritual needs that transcend the human ability to resolve.

EMBRACE THE AUTHORITY OF THE PROPHETIC

One of the strongest biblical injunctions to pray with authority is Jesus' words to His disciples to "Pray ye therefore the Lord of the harvest, that He will send forth laborers into his harvest" (Matt. 9:38). Unless we embrace the fact that prayer is spiritual, we cannot pray with authority to bring about the purposes of God.

The priority of God's heart is that no one be lost to His kingdom. Unless we go in the power of His prophetic anointing that will "open the eyes of the blind" to their deception, false gods, and spiritual darkness, we labor in vain. It is this terrible reality that should keep us waiting before the throne of God, realizing our dependency on His Spirit, and seeking His empowerment to win the lost.

I fear there are too many churches founded on good intent and the desire to help others, but based in human effort to do good things. This spiritual dimension of prayer must be embraced if we want to succeed in winning the lost. Only in the womb of prayer can spiritual births happen, resulting in the winning of souls and bringing the purposes of God to the earth.

It is a never-ending adventure to follow the leading of the Holy Spirit as He reveals His will for us through prayer. How my heart has been enlarged as I have sought to obey Him in going where He leads. Every harvest field is so different, so ripe for reaping, and so very precious to the heart of God.

My latest adventure was about to begin in a place I could never have dreamed of going—and my heart thrilled once again to be a part of the great end-time harvest in the nation of Mozambique.

If you want that splendid power in prayer, you must remain in loving, living, lasting, conscious, practical, abiding union with the Lord Jesus Christ.

—Charles H. Spurgeon[1]

CHAPTER 20

TO MOZAMBIQUE WITH LOVE

In 2009, after hearing of the remarkable work Rolland and Heidi Baker were doing in the nation of Mozambique, I decided to take a medical team to help them in their clinics. I also wanted to become personally acquainted with them and their ministry. I felt the Holy Spirit was leading me to another harvest field and that He had something to teach me there. It was simply another "chapter" in my lifelong pattern of seeking God wherever He is moving in the earth.

From what I had read about the core values of Iris Ministries, I knew that the Bakers practiced a prayer lifestyle.[2] They pursued intimate communion with Jesus as their source for the remarkable supernatural power manifest in their ministry. Heidi Baker concludes: "We do not expect fruitfulness to come out of anything but intimacy with Him."[3] Their dependency on the Holy Spirit was evident in her statement: "We also need His anointing to accomplish anything."[4]

❧

"We do not expect fruitfulness to come out of anything but intimacy with Him."
—Heidi Baker

❧

After the team and I arrived, I engaged Rolland and Heidi in conversation regarding their ministry to evangelize this nation for Christ. Rolland told me that after serving as missionaries to the poor in China and England for twenty years, they were discouraged by the little fruit that they had seen, and they no longer wanted to preach a gospel with limited results. They began to seek God for His supernatural power to set captives free. As a result, their prayer lives deepened, and they moved into a new intimacy with God. They spent more time in soaking prayer and among the poor.

Then Rolland related how miracles began to happen among these syncretistic tribes of another faith. He said the deaf are hearing, the blind are seeing, babies are healed of AIDS, and even the dead are being raised. As a result, whole villages began to turn from Islam to Christ.

After twelve years in Mozambique, God's supernatural provision (they do not ask for help from anyone) has helped them establish 10,000 churches and facilities and workers to care for more than 10,000 orphans. Through the divine power released through intimate relationship with God, they have learned to expect Him to hear their cry. And they are receiving His supernatural intervention, divine protection, and financial provision.

INTIMACY WITH CHRIST RELEASES MIRACLE POWER

In an article called "Enjoying Our God," Rolland writes about the impetus that personal relationship with God is to their ongoing success in presenting Christ in Mozambique:

> After thirty years of missionary work, Heidi and I understand more than ever that God wants to be our greatest pleasure. Our whole aim as Christians, according to the Westminster Shorter Catechism, is "to glorify God and to enjoy Him forever". For us this finds expression particularly through ministry to the poor, and to "the least of these." We do this through the grace of God and the power of the Holy Spirit.

[Here in Mozambique] the poor come to Jesus whole villages at a time because they see the power of God's love. We are financed because God grants supernatural generosity to thousands of people without appeals from us. Heidi and I would both be dead now without miraculous healing. We face need, pain and suffering every day that cry out for more than any human can give. We are made for God. We are made for revival. We are made for the glory of His Presence. We must encounter Him.[5]

> **"We are made for revival. We are made for the glory of His Presence."**
> **—Rolland Baker**

The Bakers have experienced the multiplication of food on many occasions when there was not enough prepared for the number of people who appeared. And healing the deaf has become a part of the strategy the Lord has given them for converting whole villages to Jesus. Weekly, they plan outreaches to villages where the gospel has never been preached. They take some of their older children with them, who have learned to pray like they do, along with medical doctors and other workers. They often go into a village and first show the love of Jesus through offering medical aid, treating sickness and disease among the people who live there.

After treating the sick, the leaders call for a meeting to tell the villagers about Christ. Then they request any who are deaf to come to receive prayer to the true God who will heal them. When the deaf are healed, the entire village accepts Christ, acknowledging the power of this God who has healed one of their own. Immediately, another church is formed around this miraculous demonstration of God's love in healing the deaf.

HANDS-ON HARVEST

When I visited their ministry, I had the opportunity to go with the Bakers on one of their outreaches to a previously unreached village. I soon realized how seriously devoted they are to prayer as they prepare for these outreaches. They invited me to a doctor's home the night before. There we spent four hours in fervent prayer. We asked for our own empowerment, believing God for the faithfulness of His presence, protection, and provision for the journey. We asked for souls to be won to the kingdom of Christ and for miracles of His love to reach these darkened hearts.

The next day, we boarded a truck with the team and supplies needed for reaching a new village. After driving for several hours, we arrived at a clearing, and our work began. The Iris Ministries workers quickly erected a tent for the medical team to minister to those who would come from the village for treatment.

As I looked around, I noticed about twenty-five men standing under a large tree just a few yards away. I wanted to go speak with them and tell them about Jesus, but all the interpreters were busy at the moment.

So I turned to a young Mozambican man whom I had heard speak a little English. Hopeful, I encouraged him, "You can be my interpreter to tell those men over there about Jesus."

He looked at me horrified. "No, Mama, not speak much English, only little," he answered politely. I smiled and asked my reluctant interpreter to come with me. He complied, and we strolled over to the men.

Of all the stories I could have told, I found myself sharing with them the story of the Gadarene demoniac (see Mark 8). When I finished the story, not knowing how much was actually interpreted, I said to them simply, "Jesus will set you free from your demons, too." When I said that, they began to look at each other. After they asked one of the men in their group a couple of questions, they nodded to me that they had understood.

Twelve of those men raised their hands to receive Jesus. Some with alcohol on their breath quietly acknowledged, "I know I have demons. I want Jesus to take them away."

Then to my amazement, the man who had answered their questions stepped forward. In perfect English he said, "Thank you, Mama. You have clearly explained what Jesus will do. Now we can all be free."

What a joy it was to pray with them and know that, once again, the Holy Spirit had led me to say and do the right thing to reap this wonderful harvest. Love for these people filled my heart and gave me a desire to see them come to Christ. In spite of the rugged, jungle conditions, I was filled with inexplicable joy to be in another harvest field.

I witnessed a deaf girl healed there, which prompted the village to accept Christ as the true God and Healer. It was such a joy to give my testimony of what Jesus had done for me. To recount, in the simplest terms, my story of how lost I was until Jesus came into my life renewed my awe of the saving power of God. Watching the Holy Spirit open hearts to His love is one of the greatest joys we can know this side of heaven.

I can still feel the exhilaration of riding home in the back of a truck with a large group of Mozambican children and workers. I looked at the millions of stars in the black Mozambican sky, thanking God that another village had come to Jesus. As the team sang praises to God the entire time, I wept over the love that I felt for this nation. Surely, I thought, I will return many times and bring teams to help to reap this harvest.

I did not know how the enemy would try to thwart that desire to be a part of this harvest. His life-threatening plan would hinder me from returning to Mozambique for some time. But it would ultimately work for my good in leading me ever deeper into the presence of God through prayer. Greater revelation of the enemy's tactics and deepened trust in the delivering power of God awaited me in the coming months.

Prayer breaks all bars, dissolves all chains, opens all prisons, and widens all straits by which God's saints have been held.

—E.M. Bounds[1]

Prayer is never wrestling with God, but wrestling with the powers of darkness. The "unjust judge" is not a picture of God. Our heavenly Father wants to answer us.

—John Follette[2]

CHAPTER 21

LEARNING THROUGH SUFFERING

WHEN YOU READ THE WORD of God, have you ever wondered what happened between the great miracles of deliverance, the healings, and the great sermons preached? Do you think about what daily life was like for Moses as Israel wandered through the wilderness for forty years? What were King David's ordinary days like? Or what about the apostles, who were experiencing mighty miracles while establishing the Church?

In our own lives, we tend to think about the high points when God did a wonder, answered our prayers, and directed us by His Spirit. Of course, it is that testimony of what He has done in our lives that brings glory to God. Yet not all of life is lived from mountain peak to mountain peak. We do have to descend into the valleys between in order to reach the next wonder that God performs. And we have to live every day that God gives to us in faith and trust, whether the days seem grand or ordinary.

Throughout this book, I have shared mainly the "mountain peaks" of the wonderful ways the Holy Spirit has taught me to pray. From the day of my salvation experience, prayer has been my divine classroom. It has become a lifestyle where my relationship with God has been forged daily.

But there are other classrooms as well—perplexing situations, difficult relationships, grief over the loss of a loved one, and circumstances of life that take place on those ordinary days. Still, without prayer, how can we hope to interpret the situations of life, good or bad? It is the Holy Spirit who renews our minds and teaches us how to confront life in every situation.

I have given testimony to some of the high points of my life and ministry in an effort to inspire you to deepen your life of prayer. I am keenly aware that the lessons I have learned through prayer are responsible for whatever fruitfulness has been produced in my Christian walk. Those mountain peak experiences are my encouragement to pursue God, even in the valleys.

Yet, there are lessons, perhaps more powerful, certainly more personal, that the Holy Spirit has taught me in the low points of my life. Sometimes we are more ready to learn when we are hurting than when all is well. As the wisest man of all time mused: "Sorrow is better than laughter, for sadness has a refining influence on us" (Eccles. 7:3 NLT).

It has been in times of deepest suffering that I have been aware of an infusion of compassion for others and of my dependence on the grace of God. The mystery of suffering is best understood, I think, by the promise of the apostle Paul, "And we know that all things work together for good to them that love God, to them who are the called according to his purpose" (Rom. 8:28).

My Perplexing Dilemma

Recently, I was challenged to deepen my devotional prayer life due to a painful physical condition. After returning from my wonderful ministry in Mozambique, I began to experience alarming symptoms in my body. It began with pain in my fingers and arm.

Then the pain and swelling moved to other joints in my hands and knees, making it difficult to walk. Eventually, I suffered neuropathy in my legs and feet so that I was confined to a wheelchair and scooter for a few months. Coupled with alarming weight loss, I knew this was no passing "virus." I asked my intercessors to pray for me. And I decided to visit my doctor for a possible diagnosis.

I have known very little sickness in my life. The Scriptures teach us to practice stewardship of our bodies, which are the temple of the Holy Ghost (see I Cor. 3:16). One of my priorities in life has been to trust God for "divine health" so that I can be able to do the work of God effectively.

To that end, I have established a lifestyle of eating nutritionally, exercising, fasting regularly, resting, and caring for my body as a temple of the Holy Ghost. As a result of God's faithfulness, I have been able to travel to the nations, with the rigors involved, and function normally. Except for fatigue and the occasional bout of dysentery, I have not experienced any serious ill effects during my travels abroad. Occasional cold or flu symptoms were the extent of illness I had experienced.

So, I felt ambushed after my return from Mozambique, as I began suffering the pain and symptoms of a "mysterious" illness. Their crippling effects from the neuropathy in my feet, swelling of joints, and excruciating pain would last for a number of months. Doctors were at a loss to definitively diagnose my condition. They prescribed pain medicine and little else.

Jesus Understands Our "Lapses"

As a result of the severe, ongoing pain and the side effects of the medications, I was not myself. I was struggling to cope with my physical distress as well as the mental quandary of why this was happening—and the questions of how it would end. The tentative prognosis given by the doctors was not very encouraging.

The incomprehensible origin of this physical ordeal, along with the sheer intensity of the battle, exhausted me mentally and spiritually. This struggle resulted in a faltering of my devotional prayer life. Though I was acutely aware of my need to feel close to Jesus, I did not. I lacked both the energy and motivation to wait on the Lord.

As a result, I lost that precious sense of His presence on which I had grown to depend daily since I had become a Christian. I was accustomed to a lifestyle of communion with the Lord. Yet now, when it seemed I needed Him most, I felt the least capable of pressing into His presence.

FINDING HIS COMFORT

During this "valley" experience, I found comfort in that famous poem, "Footprints in the Sand."[3] You may be familiar with this classic poem, in which the author relates a dream she had of walking on a beach with the Lord. As she looked at the pathway they had walked, her life passed before her. She recalled the events of her life and saw that during the hardest trials of her life, there was only one set of footprints in the sand.

Assuming those footprints were hers, she asked the Lord why He would not have walked beside her when she needed Him most. He responded kindly that the one set of footprints she saw during those difficult times of her life were His. For those were the times He carried her in His strong arms.

Reading that poem with fresh eyes, I was comforted to think that for some months there must have been only one set of footprints in the sand. Though I was unaware of His presence, I knew that Jesus and I had "walked" together through my terrible ordeal. The morning finally came when I brought my hungry heart to Him and wept bitterly.

I cried, "Lord, You know where I've been. I'm so sorry I couldn't do any better. I don't know where I would be if my friends hadn't prayed for me during this time when I have been overwhelmed in my illness. Please take me back and help me feel close to You again. I need You so much."

In that moment, my heart melted and I felt alive to Him again. The tears flowed freely, and my spirit was deeply comforted. I cried, "Take me back, Jesus. Please take me back." And from that morning, the relationship of communion with Jesus on which I had learned to depend was restored. Though I had been oblivious to His presence, He had "carried" me it seemed. Rather than distancing Himself from me, as I had felt, He had held me close to Himself.

I am not saying that I questioned my salvation during this ordeal; that was never a consideration. But our destiny and privilege is to commune and fellowship with God continually. He wants us to daily enjoy fellowship, comfort, and divine love in His presence. Our hearts will always be desperate and unfulfilled without that "manifest" relationship of His presence to our souls.

SEEKING DIRECTION FOR MY HEALING

One of the first places I looked for answers to my health crisis was within my own heart. I believe that we can open a door to the enemy if we have hidden sin in our hearts. I asked the Holy Spirit to shine His light on any unforgiveness or other sinful heart condition. Where I felt His conviction, I went to individuals to make sure we were walking in the light with each other. It was a time of deep soul searching and contrition, waiting on God to "create in me a clean heart," as the psalmist prayed (Ps. 51:10).

Then, because the doctors could not arrive at a satisfactory diagnosis themselves, I began to seek the Lord for His direction regarding this mysterious illness. I was desirous of a supernatural miracle in a moment of time. Barring that result, I needed to find some answers. The Holy Spirit was faithful again to help me confront this perplexing situation.

No stranger to natural health remedies, I began to research possible avenues of natural healing that would restore the use of my limbs. Under strict supervision of professionals, I began an intensive detoxification program that would rid my system of foreign bacteria and other toxins.

I felt a real measure of relief from this program after several weeks of cleansing my system. I also worked with a specialist for curing neuropathy using controlled electric current to "wake up" the nerves. I experienced good results from that therapy as well. But the pain, loss of appetite, and continued weight loss told me that we had not found the entire answer for my ongoing condition.

CHALLENGING THE DEVIL IN PRAYER

During those months that I suffered from this mysterious illness, I preached the Word every Sunday from a sitting position. The congregation was upholding me in prayer and in many other ways. I continued to serve the church as much as possible, though I had to delegate much of my responsibility to my pastoral staff who supported me during this entire ordeal.

I was also reading books about great healing ministries documented throughout history, asking the Holy Spirit to show me how to receive the healing I so desperately needed. Valid healing ministries that are functioning today were next on my list. In my pursuit, I happened to come across the name of Ana Mendez Ferrell of Mexico.

Ana and her husband, Emerson, are founders of Ambassador Ministries. They minister in more than forty nations, teaching Christians to tear down strongholds of evil and usher in the glory of God.[4]

Ana was converted to Jesus from "the profound miseries" of serving Satan as a high priestess of voodoo magic. She lost her sanity for a time as a result. Yet God in His great mercy rescued her as she called on His name. Her deliverance reads like that of the demoniac that Jesus rescued when He walked the earth (see Luke 8:26-35). Through her deep psychological trauma and bondage, from which she was miraculously delivered through faith in Christ, she developed a great compassion for anyone bound by the devil's wicked power.

I called her office, and she and her husband kindly invited me to a conference they were leading in Florida. Barely able to make the flight with the help of my travel companion, I arrived at the meeting in a wheelchair, suffering great discomfort.

Yet I was immediately aware that I had entered an atmosphere of powerful love and faith. After a lengthy time of intense praise and worship, Ana began to lead prayers directed by the Holy Spirit to set captives free. She seemed oblivious of the people, yet was interceding for them as if she knew each one. Many in the large audience began to weep; the love of God flowed over my own heart as I sat there basking in His presence.

DELIVERANCE FROM SATANIC CAPTIVITY

Do we realize how intent the devil is on his mission to "kill, steal, and destroy" (John 10:10)? If we did, I think our prayer lives would quickly become more fervent. I am grateful that when we face the enemy's cruel tactics, we can be confident that deliverance from the powers of darkness is God's will. According to the Scriptures, it is why Jesus came to earth.

The Spirit of the Lord is upon me, because he hath anointed me to preach the gospel to the poor; he hath sent me to heal the brokenhearted, to preach deliverance to the captives, and recovering of sight to the blind, to set at liberty them that are bruised (Luke 4:18).

...For this purpose the Son of God was manifested, that he might destroy the works of the devil (1 John 3:8).

The devil is a liar, the father of lies. He will continually try to get us to accept his lies to hold us in bondage to his will, which is to destroy the work of God in our lives. We cannot be successful ministers of Jesus while we are ourselves held in some type of bondage. We must seek God to walk in the abundant life He came to bring to us.

PROPHETIC REVELATION IN PRAYER

I experienced the first symptoms of my illness in South Africa, where I taught the conference on worship before continuing on my way to work in Mozambique with Rolland and Heidi Baker. Some of my prophetic mentors in ministry were convinced that the illness I was suffering was an attack of the enemy against my ministry in the nations.

I realized that when I went to Mozambique, I had entered a territory where Satan was losing his stronghold over a nation. The potential for major conflict with the enemy's forces is far greater in a territory where Satan is being challenged through applying the authority of the victory of Calvary. While the cause of my symptoms might prove to be "natural," I believe the source of the illness was indeed spiritual.

Ana Ferrell arranged a private time when she and her prayer team would minister to me for my healing. I had not told them specifics of my physical condition or the circumstances of its onset. So you can imagine my comfort when she began to share the revelation she received in prayer regarding my condition.

She said, "I see Satan plotting to attack you in South Africa. His hatred toward you is fierce. He has his demon helpers form the attack. They bind your ankles, your knees, and your wrists. I perceive that their hatred is satisfied as they put you in bondage." Those were the specific areas of my body that had been the most affected by my illness.

As Ana and her team prayed for me, she exercised her faith to "pull me out of this region of captivity" perpetrated by the evil one. It was like taking a giant leap forward out of the clutches of the enemy. Rarely had I felt such depths of compassion as I received through Ana and her prayer team. My heart was melted by the love of God that flowed through their prayers.

Afterward, I felt a tremendous release in my inner person and a peace in my body and mind that I had not felt in months. I was stronger physically from that moment and experienced an easing of the symptoms that had crippled me for months.

Even in this "classroom" of prayer, the Holy Spirit was leading me into a greater dimension of Jesus' wonderful healing love. Through my experiencing of such deep compassion and divine authority over the enemy, He was teaching me how to pray for others. There are places of satanic captivity from which we need to set captives free by faith. He is a liar, but when we know the truth, we can be set free.

LEARNING TO WALK IN DIVINE HEALING

Life became easier as peace returned to my mind and heart. I was gaining strength, and hope was springing up that there would be an end to this lengthy season of affliction. I continued to make physical progress and felt a new sense of emotional well-being. My friends saw the progress and rejoiced with me.

I was walking again and gaining weight. The swelling in my joints and the neuropathy were disappearing gradually. I began to travel in ministry again, and I continued to seek God for complete healing from the remaining debilitating symptoms of illness.

The Lord helped me to minister the truths I was learning about healing to my congregation and to other churches where I ministered. We saw supernatural victories in their lives as a result. Once again, I rejoiced in the fulfillment of the promise that "all things work together for good" (Rom. 8:28) when we seek to walk in the purposes of God for our lives.

YOU HAVE TO FIGHT

Heidi Baker was scheduled to minister in a conference at Shekinah during this season of my recovery. When I spoke with her in private, I asked her to talk with me about what they had learned about divine healing.

Heidi shared with me some dramatic healings she and her husband had received during their thirty years as missionaries. In each situation,

God worked differently to effect their healing. They had to obey the particular instructions the Holy Spirit gave to receive their healing.

For example, when she was diagnosed with multiple sclerosis, she asked friends in ministry to pray. She received e-mails from two ministers telling her that medical studies showed a link between multiple sclerosis and a particular artificial sweetener. Heidi had been using that sweetener. When she received that news, she quit using it. Within six weeks, she was free from all symptoms of multiple sclerosis!

On another occasion, Heidi was in the hospital with incurable staph infection that was not responding to treatment. Doctors feared for her life; the prognosis was grim. As she lay there with IVs in her arm asking God to heal her, she felt impressed that she should keep a preaching appointment in Canada.

To the consternation of doctors and friends, she checked herself out of the hospital and made the arduous trip to Canada. She was so ill that she could hardly climb the steps to the platform. She was simply walking in obedience to the command of the Holy Spirit. And when she stood to minister, she felt the power of God flood her body. In that moment, she was completely healed from this life-threatening condition.

She had taken her running shoes with her to Canada in faith that she would need them. The morning after her healing, she put her shoes on and went outside to jog. When her friends saw her, they were concerned and felt they needed to caution her. "Don't you think this is too soon to be jogging considering how seriously ill you have been?"

Smiling at them kindly, Heidi asked: "What is there about *healed* that you don't understand?"

Heidi's husband, Rolland, was dying of what doctors had diagnosed as a dementia-related illness. He had suffered for months and doctors could not find any treatment that helped to bring improvement. Finally, when they felt death was imminent, they told Heidi to call the family in to say their goodbyes.

When Rolland's good friend, Mel Tari, a great revivalist and author of *Like a Mighty Wind,*[5] heard the grave news, he called them. He asked if he could take Rolland to a Christian healing center in another country. It was established specifically to minister to the sick through prayer along with practical medical help. It seemed too late for such a trip, but they agreed to let him go. Rolland recovered completely after a few months of treatment and intense prayer that he received daily in that center.

RESISTING THE DEVIL

Heidi's personal exhortation to me was simple: "Sue, you have to fight for your healing." She continued to explain how they have had to challenge the devil in prayer, pronouncing his defeat through the cross of Christ. She admitted that they have lost battles in Mozambique, but she said they are winning the war.

My conversation with Heidi confirmed what the Holy Spirit was teaching me about challenging the devil in prayer for my healing. And the Holy Spirit had been faithful to reveal specific instructions for me to receive total healing. Through prayer, He had led me to employ some "natural" means and had led me to people who could pray with revelation of the root cause in order to defeat the enemy's plan for my physical demise.

I understood that there is a time to challenge the devil and command the works of darkness and the ravages of sickness to leave a person's life. In Jesus' ministry, He often rebuked a devil and commanded the infirmity to leave a person.

These lessons concerning healing were welcome to me. They were more powerful than just intellectual knowledge or shared experiences. Because of my own suffering, I needed to embrace them in faith and walk in the truth of them. As I did, I was experiencing healing through obedience to each portion of truth the Holy Spirit revealed.

Yet it seemed that the Holy Spirit had more to teach; the end of this "painful semester" was not yet. He would lead me to witness other powerful ministries of healing and rejoice with extraordinary miracles that were happening before my eyes.

We can do nothing without prayer. All things can be done by importunate prayer. That is the teaching of Jesus Christ.

—E.M. Bounds[1]

CHAPTER 22

MORE LESSONS IN HEALING

B Y NOW, THE NEUROPATHY I had suffered was greatly improved and
normal feeling was returning to my legs and feet. My hands and
arms were functioning almost normally, and I was gaining energy
daily. Yet there were still some residual symptoms of the illness. I was
determined to experience complete restoration from this vile attack of
the enemy on my body. I need to be completely free from sickness so
that I could function normally to accomplish the work of God.

I heard that Norvel Hayes was ministering in a nearby city. Founder
of New Life Bible College, he is well known for his healing and miracle
services.[2] My husband and I decided to attend these services. We were
aware that we were still learning lessons the Holy Spirit was teaching
regarding healing.

There was a beautiful, intense time of worship to begin the service.
Pastor Hayes teaches the priority of praise to enter into the presence of
God. In fact, his mission statement says: "The vision of our ministry is
to teach and train individuals how to know God through true worship
and to build in them a strong foundation of the Word of God."

After worship, as he taught the Word, Pastor Hayes pointed out
several places in the Scriptures where people were healed after first
worshiping Jesus. Then he said, "If you will worship first, you can ask
the Lord for anything."

I listened intently that morning as he ministered the Word. He also taught another biblical principle, which is vitally linked with worship: the principle of giving. He read from the Scriptures:

> *Give unto the Lord the glory due unto his name: bring an offering, and come into his courts. O worship the Lord in the beauty of holiness: fear before him, all the earth* (Psalm 96:8-9).

How often do believers fail to equate giving with worship? Some simply consider they are paying the church bills or helping the needy. According to the Scriptures, giving monetarily is as much an act of worship as bowing before the Lord in heartfelt adoration.

As I mentioned, I have taught the principles of giving to my church regarding the scriptural pattern of bringing tithes and offerings. We understand that obedience in giving allows God to "open the windows of heaven, and pour you out a blessing, that there shall not be room enough to receive it" (Mal. 3:10).

After his sermon, Pastor Hayes gave an invitation for prayer for healing. I went forward to receive prayer. Before praying for me, based on his commitment to his message that day, he asked me publicly, "Did you bring an offering today?"

You can imagine my relief when I could respond, "Yes, sir."

I do not believe in embracing legalistic "rules" for receiving a miracle from God; we certainly do not "buy" His favor as some have errone-ously taught through Church history. Yet according to the Scriptures, it is true that as our hearts are open to love God and obey His Word, His blessings can be poured into our lives.

In fact, all of God's promises, in both the Old and New Testaments, are for those who seek Him with their whole hearts. That is because, above all else, God created humankind to walk in a love relationship with Him. It is in this intimate relationship with the Lord that we truly touch Him to receive wholeness for our lives, just as the woman did who touched the hem of His garment so long ago (see Matt. 9:20).

Once again, I felt strengthened by the healing power of God through Norvel Hayes' prayer. I was encouraged that God was leading me step-by-step on this journey to complete restoration of my health. And in the process, He was confirming truths in which we had walked, such as praise and worship and giving. There are dimensions to every truth, and as we grow in God, we can expect to receive greater empowerment to walk in them.

More Miracles to Increase Our Faith

A few weeks later, I heard about a wonderful outpouring of signs and wonders happening in a revival in Daphne, Alabama. It was happening in the church of our friend, Pastor John Kilpatrick, who ministers in our conferences at Shekinah. He had invited a young evangelist named Nathan Morris from England to minister for a conference in his church.[3] Nathan laughingly says, "I came for two days and have stayed for four months"…and counting. Because God was touching His people in tangible, life-changing ways, they continued the meetings indefinitely.

What drew me to visit the revival was hearing of the miraculous healing of Delia Knox, a pastor's wife who had been paralyzed for twenty-three years. A drunken driver struck her car, and Delia's spine was broken; she had not walked since the accident. All those years, Delia was seeking God for healing and had been prayed for numerous times. She had become so weary in her struggle that, at times, she tried to simply accept her condition as irreversible. But God had other plans for her.

Because she was the wife of a local pastor, the news of her healing traveled the nation like wildfire. And because of the marvel of video and internet, people could watch her get up out of her wheelchair and begin to walk on her own after twenty-three years of paralysis.

Numerous other documented miracles of healing followed. A young boy was healed of a malignant brain tumor. They brought x-rays of his head before and after from his doctor, who could only affirm a miraculous intervention in reversing the boy's condition.

As my husband, John, and I sat in those meetings, I could only weep as we witnessed personally the healing of a woman hopelessly crippled with rheumatoid arthritis. She described her pitiful existence before her healing. She had to give up her nursing career because of this disability. She could no longer walk or even use her hands. She was dependent on the help of others to do the simplest tasks that require the use of hands and legs.

This woman was so desperate to be healed that she had borrowed money from a friend and traveled on a plane, alone, as an invalid in a wheelchair, scarcely able to clutch her purse. Upon her arrival in Daphne, she had asked a total stranger to help her get to the church.

This was not her first trip in search of the healing she so desperately needed. She had recently returned from Nigeria, where she had heard God was healing people. There, Christians who prayed for her told her that it simply was not her time to be healed. Imagine the sense of hopelessness she must have felt.

And now that word of hopelessness had been reversed! We witnessed the power of God release her limbs from that crippling condition. She could walk again, bend over backward and forward, and even run! She could lift her arms above her head and wave them and use her hands normally. She no longer needed her wheelchair. During the meeting the next evening, we saw her walking around the large sanctuary as a perfectly normal woman.

More Holy Spirit "Classroom" Time

I had come to this conference seeking to understand the moving of the Holy Spirit in healing power. *What does the Holy Spirit want to teach me here?* Once again, I joined in a lengthy worship service preceding the ministry of the Word. I understood the vital importance of sincere worship, which prepares the atmosphere for miracles.

Every service of this conference began with heartfelt worship that would last about an hour and a half. I observed that the worshipers were committed to loving God and expressing that love with a focused intensity. Worship leaders and musicians set the tone of loving surrender to His Lordship as they exalted God alone through song.

The power of worship cannot be overemphasized. I concur with many Bible scholars who teach that an act of worship is the highest level of prayer. It is the creature's proper response to the Creator, the believer's humble gratitude expressed to their Savior. It is the response of God to our poured-out love for Him. In that place of intimate communion, spirit-to-Spirit, God releases His power to heal and to eradicate every destructive effect of sin.

We left those powerful services, where the presence of God reduced us to weeping and lifted us to new heights of praise, with increased faith for what God is doing in the earth today. There is nothing like witnessing miracles happening through prayer and worship to enlarge your heart to receive from Him.

As I shared the wonderful testimonies of the miracles we witnessed with our congregation, their faith was also strengthened. New desires to press into God in prayer are the result of seeing the power of God in action. We are encouraged to believe God for the personal and corporate needs we share when we have witnessed the love of God to give miracles of healing to His children.

There is no end to the "classroom" instruction of the Holy Spirit. All my life, He has been teaching me to pray. Yet, I am aware that there are dimensions of prayer that I have not yet reached. There is a demonstration of His power to establish His kingdom in the earth that we have not yet experienced. We must never settle for life in God as we have known it. It is the desire of my heart to grow in faith and love for God continually until I see Him face-to-face.

Prayers are deathless. They outlive the lives of those who pray them.

—E.M. Bounds[1]

Prayer is my chief work, and it is by means of it that I carry on the rest.

—Thomas Hooker, Puritan[2]

CHAPTER 23

SCHOOL ISN'T OUT YET

I ONCE HEARD NORVEL HAYES say, "Faith can't tell time." That is a powerful statement regarding one of our greatest enemies to faith: delay. We want God to answer our prayers immediately. When He doesn't, we often become discouraged or, worse, unbelieving.

Perseverance is a powerful biblical truth that we must embrace to see the results we want to receive through prayer. This powerful virtue is evident in the lives of the Old Testament patriarchs like Abraham. He "hoped against hope" for the fulfillment of God's covenant promises. Jesus also taught the imperative of perseverance, as in the parable of the unjust judge:

> And he spake a parable unto them to this end, that men ought always to pray, and not to faint; saying, There was in a city a judge, which feared not God, neither regarded man: And there was a widow in that city; and she came unto him, saying, Avenge me of mine adversary. And he would not for a while: but afterward he said within himself, Though I fear not God, nor regard man; Yet because this widow troubleth me, I will avenge her, lest by her continual coming she weary me...And shall not God avenge his own elect, which cry day and night unto him, though he bear long with them? (Luke 18:1-5, 7)

Faith will keep asking because God's Word has to be true. We must learn to persevere in prayer if we are to prevail over the persevering tactics of the evil one. The time factor cannot be underestimated in its power to discourage and defeat Christians in their pursuit of God's promises.

Many times, our faith wavers because we think we know when and how God should answer our prayers. For example, we seek healing and expect an instantaneous miracle, rather than allowing the Holy Spirit to lead us into divine healing.

Smith Wigglesworth, who enjoyed remarkable miracles in his ministry, concluded, "God rejoices when we manifest a faith that holds Him to His Word."[3] With no time limit and no preconceived notions, we must just trust that God's Word is true.

God's Word promises healing, and when we "hold Him to His Word," He delights to fulfill it in our lives. Even if that fulfillment does not happen in an instant, we must exercise our faith to believe His Word until we have what we asked.

FAITH TRANSCENDS TIME

I shared the testimony of Delia Knox, who was miraculously healed in the Bay of the Holy Spirit Revival in 2010 after twenty-three years of paralysis.[4] After her accident, she and her husband had continued to pastor, their faith sorely tried by the injustice of this life-changing event. She testified to her struggle with discouragement and her efforts to continue to believe God for her healing. We can only imagine the triumphant joy they felt when they received their miracle after so long a time.

Yet even after her miracle began, there was a time element involved. The first night Delia was prayed for during this recent revival, she had feeling return to her legs. For the first time in twenty-three years, when she grasped her legs, she could feel her fingers running up and down them. Convinced that something supernatural was happening, she took a few labored steps, engaging her still atrophied muscles with help.

Then she was pushed out of the service in her wheelchair one more time. Though it was obvious to Delia that healing had begun, it would not be an instantaneous miracle. Her faith would be tested again during the next few days to believe for completion of what God had begun.

A few nights later, she received more prayer and was able to move her legs more vigorously and walk with less help. A week later, she again received prayer at the revival meeting. This time she walked freely; her healing was accomplished.

John and I visited the revival a month after that and saw Delia walking normally, wearing stiletto heels. We rejoiced with her as she walked the platform, ministering in song to the Lord. Someone asked her, "Why stiletto heels?"

Delia's response was, "I wore stilettos before I lost the use of my legs; why wouldn't I wear them now?"

When I spoke with her, she confirmed that her complete healing had taken a few weeks, but that now she is walking as if she had not been paralyzed for twenty-three years. Once again, faith had transcended time.

Faith can't tell time; in the end, it must transcend time to receive the fulfillment of God's promises. Abraham is the man of record for this core reality of faith. God gave him a wonderful promise, complete with the magnitude of His purposes for Abraham's progeny. There was only one problem; the years went by without any progeny appearing. In human terms, it was simply too late to receive such a promise. Yet even then, Abraham's faith transcended the "time" factor in order to receive the long-awaited promise of God in Isaac:

For what saith the scriptures? Abraham believed God, and it was counted unto him for righteousness...(As it is written, I have made thee a father of many nations,) before him whom he believed, even God, who quickeneth the dead, and calleth those things which be not as thought they were. Who against hope believed in hope, that he might become the father of many nations, according to that which was spoken, So shall thy seed be...He staggered not at the promise of God through unbelief; but was strong in faith, giving glory to God (Romans 4:3, 17-18, 20).

AFTER YEARS OF SERVICE

Rolland and Heidi Baker shared with me that they were discouraged after years of missionary work because of a lack of results. Their faith was being tried by the element of time, in this case years, without seeing the fulfillment of God's Word for the harvest of souls they desired. Yet in God's economy, those years were not wasted. They served to test the faith of this missionary family and press them into the supernatural power for which they longed. Rolland describes the supernatural source of their success in Mozambique as a result of the triumph of their faith over the test of time. God answered their cry to experience "a gospel that worked":

> All the good work we have been able to do in this movement in Africa has been sparked, fueled and sustained by the fire of revival and the supernatural…. We do what we do because of visitations, visions and heavy doses of His Spirit. We are excited and keep going because the dead are being raised and the blind and deaf are being healed.[5]

I learned from the Bakers some of the devil's strategies that they had faced in Mozambique. They had not raised up thousands of churches in this nation and enough facilities and workers to care for 10,000 orphans without learning how to successfully challenge the devil in prayer. I was impressed by the fact that they do not ask for funds for their ministry; rather, they seek God in prayer for His supernatural provision to accomplish His work.

Their testimonies of miracles of healing among these tribes and the broadening Christian influence they were establishing in the nation prompted a radio station to announce that northern Mozambique had "fallen to Christianity because we [Muslims] cannot compete with the opening of blind eyes and deaf ears and raising the dead."

"Write Your Tombstone"

I related earlier that Heidi Baker had been ill for months with incurable staph. She was exercising her faith against the doctors' prognosis of death. Her doctor in Africa actually said to her, "You need to write your tombstone. There is nothing that can be done." Yet, she did not accept the doctor's death sentence. She kept praying and expecting God to heal her. And when the Holy Spirit prompted her to fulfill a ministry assignment in Canada, she obeyed and was completely healed.

Through perseverance and fighting the good fight of faith, their incredible breakthrough has come to Mozambique. Time is such a weapon against faith; the enemy uses it to discourage and defeat many Christians who have not learned that faith cannot tell time.

We like the idea of instant coffee and microwavable meals. But God did not invent the microwave. We have to learn to use time as our weapon against the enemy, pressing into God's purposes and promises through prayer. As we pursue intimate relationship with the Holy Spirit, He is faithful to teach us to persevere in prayer and in faith until....

Faith must transcend time and look to eternity for the fulfillment of every promise of God in our lives. As we pursue intimate relationship with the Holy Spirit and allow Him to live in us, pray through us, and teach us all things, time will cease to be an enemy. Instead, it will become a classroom where the Holy Spirit is given pre-eminence to transform our thinking and fulfill all His will in our lives.

Living in communion with God through the Holy Spirit who dwells within us, we will be able to attain to great victories over every onslaught of the evil one. Meditating in the Word of God and abiding in Christ through prayer allows the Holy Spirit to teach us how to receive miracles that we need from God.

As our hearts are open to Him, He helps us to unlock the power He has given us to live victoriously over every tactic of the devil. Hopelessness can be turned to the exuberant joy of hope as we submit to the Lordship of Christ even when we face the terrible time test. When our faith triumphs in these situations, we are stronger and more equipped to live in victory as Christ has ordained us to.

OVERCOMING HOPELESSNESS

Hopelessness is a devastating condition; it is an emotional state in which negative circumstances and situations appear to be utterly final and seemingly irreversible. The Scriptures declare: "Hope deferred maketh the heart sick: but when the desire cometh, it is a tree of life" (Prov. 13:12). The Hebrew word translated "deferred," *mashak*, means "postponed or dragged out."[6] Sometimes when we have to wait for an answer to prayer, we can suffer from heartsickness, which is a sense of intense grief or hopelessness.

When our hope is deferred, it is a temptation to give up and cease to stand in faith because we aren't seeing the answer we need right now. It is a terrible thing to live with heartsickness, without hope. Refusing to allow time to become a defeating issue, we must choose to persevere and stand in faith *until* the answer comes. That means we hold God to His Word until we receive His wonderful promise. Faith is a condition of the heart; it cannot tell time. It simply relies on the goodness and faithfulness of God to fulfill His Word in His "eternal present."

God loves to surprise us with His miracles. That is one thing I have never quite gotten used to in my walk with God. Every day is an adventure into what God might delight to do for us that day as we allow Him to direct our steps into His ever-unfolding purposes. Yet He sometimes demands that we choose to trust Him to fulfill His promises over time, in spite of what we see with our eyes in the moment.

God knows that walking in perseverance will work for our good and bring us into more intimate relationship with Him. He allows situations that require us to wait on Him so that we can say with the psalmist, "...I trusted in thee, O Lord: I said, Thou art my God. My times are in thy hand... (Ps. 31:14-15).

Some of my most powerful lessons regarding prayer have been taught (and hopefully learned) during my months of extended illness. As I have purposed to prevail against this debilitating physical attack of the enemy in my life, it has required that I persevere in faith against what my body and mind are suffering in the moment.

People such as Heidi and Rolland Baker, who have faced life-threatening disease and prevailed through the time element to receive their miracles, have encouraged me. Witnessing miracles firsthand, such as with Delia and our friend who was healed of rheumatoid arthritis, have also inspired me to persevere in my quest for complete healing.

And the incredible faithfulness of the Holy Spirit to reveal His powerful truths regarding prayer that prevails against all the wiles of the enemy has strengthened my faith and love for God even in the midst of my trial.

No good thing was ever received by complacency, apathy, or an "if it be the Lord's will" attitude. During the past four decades, I have been privileged to interact with thousands of Christians in many nations who understand how to receive supernatural breakthroughs by learning to pray authoritatively. Every test of our faith is to be received simply as another opportunity to learn to depend on the Holy Ghost, our Divine Comforter.

THE COMFORT OF THE HOLY GHOST

In the book of Acts, after Saul was converted and ceased his murderous zeal against the churches, the Scriptures say:

Then had the churches rest throughout all Judaea and Galilee and Samaria, and were edified; and walking in the fear of the Lord, and in the comfort of the Holy Ghost, were multiplied (Acts 9:31).

The word *comfort* here is translated from the Greek word *paraklesis*, meaning "consolation, exhortation, entreaty, and encouragement."[7] The Holy Spirit has ministered to me in all of these ways. He has exhorted me to embrace His truth, entreated me to seek Him, and encouraged me that nothing is too hard for Him. I have learned that He will always be there for me. What an encouragement it is to confront all of life's challenges knowing that the Holy Spirit is there to comfort us.

I can only wonder where I would be today if the Holy Spirit did not continue His work as my Teacher to take me into new dimensions of prayer. How many enemies would still be unconquered? How many mountain peaks would never be climbed?

I love the Holy Spirit for being my teacher and for revealing Jesus to me. I love Him for letting me know Him as a Divine Person—His feelings, His mind, and His will. I am so grateful for His renewing of my mind and revealing of His will for my life. He is my faithful Companion and my Comforter.

Whether I am enjoying a mountain peak experience or enduring a journey through a valley, I am learning to rest in the confidence that the Lord is my Shepherd. He is leading me, restoring my soul, protecting me, and letting me know His "goodness and mercy" all the days of my life (see Ps. 23).

PRESENT PROGRESSIVE TENSE

As of this writing, I am still pursuing my life-long journey into greater power in prevailing prayer in order to fulfill the will of God "on earth as it is in heaven." Our church is continuing to cultivate a lifestyle of prayer, both individually and corporately. We are filled with desire to bear much fruit in the ingathering of the final harvest before Jesus comes.

My healing is almost complete; I am expecting total restoration in the near future. And my zeal for the kingdom has been strengthened through this painful ordeal rather than lessened. Lessons learned in the classroom of suffering will serve well in avoiding the attacks of the evil one. And they will motivate me to press into greater victory over the enemy in territories where he holds precious souls in bondage.

I originally titled this book, *The Holy Spirit Taught Me to Pray*, using the past tense, and its purpose was to relate the lessons I had learned in my walk with God. We understand that the spiritual lessons the Holy Spirit teaches are more accurately described in the present progressive tense. That is, they are continuing in His divine classroom in the present and into the future *until*.... Perhaps when we are ushered into His presence at the return of Jesus, our curricula will change. We can only imagine what we will be learning in that eternal present.

I readily acknowledge that I have not arrived in any sense in the ability to pray in the capacity that is available to believers. Each day, each situation in life challenges the effectiveness of our prayer lives. Yet we do not need to fear because the Holy Spirit is a faithful Teacher who guides us into all truth, moment-by-moment, in every new situation we face.

My desire has been to share with you some of the lessons I have learned in my pursuit of God through prayer. Knowing God is the meaning of life. He has given us His Holy Spirit to help us to find the meaning of life. My goal has been to inspire you, as born-again believers, that we are all students in His divinely-controlled classroom. There may be lessons in prayer you have learned for which I have not yet matriculated, and vice versa. I have learned that we can help each other along our journey toward maturity in Christ. We can encourage each other to fulfill our destiny and establish the Kingdom of God in the earth until we are ushered into eternity.

Until then, let us use time as an opportunity to know God, be led by His Spirit, and triumph over the evil one. If we let our faith transcend the test of time, we will enjoy the victory of eternity in every aspect of life. We have a faithful Teacher, the Holy Spirit, who will continually teach us to pray and to enjoy intimate relationship with our Savior, our Lord, and our soon-coming King.

If you desire a greater anointing in prayer, you may want to pray this prayer with me:

Father, I open my heart to You. I yearn to pray effective prayers. I really desire to receive answers and to know that You hear me when I pray. There are so many needs and concerns that only You can resolve.

I am so thankful that the Holy Spirit will teach us to pray. Please show me how to be led by Him in prayer. Forgive me for trying to do myself what He is here to do for me and through me. I want to be used by You in prayer. I realize that I have relied on my own thoughts rather than discovering Your will and purpose.

I ask You for a greater anointing in prayer. Please open my ears to hear Your voice. Increase my faith to begin the adventure of working and walking with You in the Spirit.

Jesus, I want to know You and to please You when I pray. You promised that if we would call unto You, You would answer. I am believing that through the power of the Holy Spirit, You will establish me as your vessel of prayer for Your glory.

In Jesus' name,

Amen.

Appendix A

BIBLICAL PRAISE EXPRESSIONS

Seven Hebrew Words for Praise[1]

I. Tehillah Meaning "praise, laudation, or hymn of praise." It is the most used word for praise in the Old Testament, coming from the word *halal*, from the root *hallelujah*. *Tehillah* is the song the Lord sings to us, through us. Christians sang *Tehillah* praise when they were being fed to the lions. It also means a fervent prayer set to music, intercession, and entreaty. Paul and Silas sang this type of praise while chained in prison, and they were delivered.	*References:* Psalm 40:3—A new song; Isaiah 60:18—"gates" is *Tehillah* (the gate into His presence is *Tehillah* praise); Isaiah 61:3—a garment of praise for a spirit of heaviness.

2. *Shabach* Meaning "praise, triumph, glory, a loud adoration, shout, proclaiming with a loud voice unashamed glory."	*References:* Psalm 145:4; Psalm 147:12—out of this shout comes triumph, actually shouting love unto God; Proverbs 29:11—to calm anger.
3. *Barak* Meaning "praise, kneel; bless, to do with motion, to use the hands or bow the knee, salute, to bless God in an act of adoration." There is usually no vocal expression in *barak* praise; the motion is bending the knee to bless the King who supplies all your needs.	*References:* Psalm 103:1; Psalm 72:15; used 330 times in the Old Testament.
4. *Halal* Meaning "praise, boast, celebrate, clamorously foolish, to rave, sing—all in an attitude of delight." When David brought the Ark of the Covenant back to Israel, he danced like a fool; it is the praise the angelic host released when announcing the birth of Jesus; Jesus came to bring *halal* praise to the Father.	*References:* Psalm 149:1; Psalm 22:22-25; Psalm 48:8; used 133 times in the Old Testament.

5. *Zamar* Meaning "praise, sing praise with the instrument, to touch with fingers the strings of an instrument, or to pluck a stringed instrument in celebration." The word *sing* is used, but it means *zamar;* it is the praise David offered when playing for Saul to rid him of the tormenting spirit.	*References:* 2 Samuel 22:50; Psalm 61:8; Psalm 66.
6. *Towdah* Meaning "praise, thank offering, to praise no matter what your circumstances; a sacrifice of praise that costs you something."	*References:* 2 Chronicles 29:31; Psalm 100:4; Psalm 50:23; Psalm 56:12.
7. *Yadah* Meaning "praise with extended hands, lifting them unashamedly to the Lord; thanksgiving, cast (throw)." When Leah had her fourth son, she raised her hands in praise to the Lord and called him Judah. This is the first mention of anyone raising hands in praise for their blessings. This praise also includes public confession of sin.	*References:* Genesis 29:35; Psalm 86:12; Psalm 108:3.

Appendix B

HINDRANCES TO CORPORATE PRAYER

Adapted from *The Praying Church* by Sue Curran[1]

1. Teaching Prayers

True praying is to "pour out your heart before him" (Ps. 62:8). That is prayer from a sincere motive. But there is also a kind of prayer that comes from people who have a point to make or some understanding they feel is too valuable to keep to themselves. A response to this problem is simply to tell the congregation, "Don't teach in your prayers. Pour out your hearts to God!"

2. Controlling Prayers

A near relative of teaching prayers, controlling prayers bring the group under the direction of a self-appointed leader. Often others are not aware the leadership has changed, but the spiritual level of the meeting soon reveals something has happened. Should this occur, those in leadership should gently redirect the flow of the meeting toward God.

3. DOCTRINAL/ATTITUDINAL PRAYERS

This kind of prayer corrects the doctrine or intention of others who have prayed. For instance, if someone has just repented in prayer, another might begin to pray, "Lord, we thank you that we have already repented. There is no condemnation. You did it all on Calvary." It may be necessary to speak with a person privately in this case to ask that person to leave the direction of the meeting to the leadership of the church.

4. EMOTIONAL PRAYERS

Wild exuberance or hysterical wailing can kill a prayer meeting. Both joy and weeping can be a part of an "alive" prayer meeting, but when those praying draw attention to themselves through excessive emotion, they are damaging the prayer meeting.

5. MORBID, UNBELIEVING PRAYERS

People must be taught that, however great or distressing their needs are, God has promised to respond to faith. It may be acceptable to weep honestly and ask for God's intervention, but it is unbelief to simply express fears and depression. Often an appropriate song can lift a meeting that has fallen under the pall of unbelief.

6. STRIVING PRAYERS

Striving simply adds pride and energy to unbelief. When people lack faith, all they can do is express their tension. They may think it unfair that God is meeting others and not them. Again, the prayer leaders must take responsibility to set a positive tone for the meeting.

7. Intellectual Prayers

Intellectual pray-ers have not learned about the spirit of prayer. They perform rehearsed prayers of their own invention. It is best to teach the people to "skip the adjectives" and simply pour out their hearts before God.

8. Dead Prayers

A cousin to intellectual prayers, these are usually spoken from throat level, never from the heart. Though the prayer meeting can usually endure a few such "underwhelming" offerings, people should be taught to pray from inspiration rather than from habit.

9. Personal, Ambitious Prayers

It is not wrong for a prayer to be personal, but there are people who use public occasions to draw attention to themselves. They pray to impress the hearers with their potential for future leadership or other personal ambitions.

10. Uncooperative Prayers

If people choose to sit when everyone is standing, pray quietly when everyone is shouting, or read their Bibles when everyone else is praying, they should understand that they are not cooperating with the prayer effort. Their personal actions are more important to them than moving in unity with the group as they pray together.

APPENDIX C

THE SEVEN OFFICES OF THE HOLY SPIRIT

Adapted from *Walking in the Anointing of the Holy Spirit*
by Fuchsia T. Pickett.[1]

The Holy Spirit as a divine Person functions in seven different spheres of service that can be called "offices." Through these offices, this Third Person of the Godhead executes specific duties to fulfill the eternal plan of God:

1. *THE SPIRIT OF LIFE* (ROMANS 8:2, 10-11)

When the Scriptures refer to the Holy Spirit as "the Spirit of...," they signify that He is the executor of the office named. For example, as the Spirit of Life, the Holy Spirit makes us alive to God by creating the life of Jesus in us. Jesus is Life (see John 14:6). The Holy Spirit is the Spirit of Life. All of the divine qualities of Jesus' life—His peace, His joy, His righteousness—reside in the Spirit of Life.

2. *THE SPIRIT OF TRUTH* (JOHN 16:13)

We cannot know God without knowing the Spirit of Truth. We cannot receive anything God has for us in the light of the Word if the Holy Spirit does not illumine it to us. Truth is a Person: Jesus Christ (see John 14:6). As we walk with the Spirit of Truth, communing with Him and yielding to Him, divine truth is ever expanding in us, bringing us to a mature relationship with God.

3. *The Spirit of Adoption* (Romans 8:15-16)

In Bible culture, the term *adoption* did not refer to people receiving an infant into their home to raise as their child. The ancient Romans and Greeks adopted no one but sons who had been born to them. When a son grew to maturity and was equipped to bear the family name responsibly, he was declared to be "a son" by his father and adopted as an heir of the family estate. *Adoption* was a recognition of mature sonship (see Gal. 4:1-2).

4. *The Spirit of Holiness* (Romans 1:3-4)

Holiness is a Person. The nature and character of the Godhead reveals true holiness. Christ Himself has become our righteousness (see 1 Cor. 1:30). Holiness is the nature of God demonstrated in our lives. True holiness is manifested by Christ-like character, not by external lifestyles. As the Spirit of Holiness, the Holy Spirit brings judgment, fire, and burning into our lives (see Isa. 10:16-18). Yet He deals with us gently, according to His nature, and gives us grace to walk in His holiness.

5. *The Spirit of Grace* (Hebrews 10:29)

The Spirit of Grace governs the attitudes and actions of the believer who has learned to walk in dependence on the Holy Spirit. Grace can be simply defined as "God's unmerited favor," His undeserved kindness. Some have called it *divine love in action.* The Spirit of Grace is the One who gives us the divine enabling to do all the Scriptures require of us and to obey God fully.

6. THE SPIRIT OF SUPPLICATION (Zechariah 12:10)

Please see explanation in text on page 131

7. THE SPIRIT OF GLORY (1 PETER 4:14)

In the Old Testament, the glory of human achievement is an ascribed glory. The glory of God is objective; it is rooted in His very nature, not in the evaluation of others. The glory of God will be revealed in us as we are victorious in the trials we must endure (see Rom. 8:18). The apostle Paul described many difficult trials he was experiencing and declared, "For momentary, light affliction is producing for us an eternal weight of glory far beyond all comparison" (2 Cor. 4:17 NASB).

GREAT AWAKENINGS IN OUR NATION

FIRST GREAT AWAKENING

The First Great Awakening was the most sweeping and transforming movement of the eighteenth century in our nation. Jonathan Edwards, who preached the famous sermon, "Sinners in the Hands of an Angry God," was one of the most influential preachers. The revival fires were ignited by the great orator, George Whitfield, from England. He preached individual salvation by faith in Christ rather than collective salvation as part of the Church of England. The revival began in the early 1700s and lasted half a century.[1]

Other preachers enjoyed powerful visitations of the Spirit of God. Barton Stone, at the invitation of Daniel Boone, preached and served at the Cane Ridge Meeting House in Bourbon County, Kentucky. Stone was so overwhelmed by the Red River revival that he went home and, in May 1801, called for a similar meeting in Cane Ridge. A second meeting, a six-day camp meeting in August, was then called. To the surprise of everyone, over 20,000 people arrived for the camp meeting.

In the words of Barton Stone,

Many, very many, fell down as men slain in battle, and continued for hours together in an apparently breathless and motionless state...sometimes uttering a deep groan, or piercing shriek, or by prayer for mercy most fervently uttered...[2]

Twenty years after Cane Ridge, Charles Finney, a lawyer called by God, came on the scene, and thousands were converted under his fiery ministry. He was followed by revivalists such as Phoebe Palmer, R.A. Torrey, A.B. Simpson, and Dwight Moody.[3]

SECOND GREAT AWAKENING

By the end of the eighteenth century, many educated Americans no longer professed traditional Christian beliefs. Revival began to spread west with new religious fervor. In western New York, the spirit of revival encouraged the emergence of new denominations. In the Appalachian region of Kentucky and Tennessee, the Methodists and the Baptists found new vigor through the revival, and a new form of religious expression was born—the camp meeting. The American Bible Society was founded in 1816. Social activism, inspired by the revival, gave rise to anti-slavery abolition groups, as well as the Society for the Promotion of Temperance.[4]

ENDNOTES

Chapter 1: Having Trouble Praying?

1. John Wesley, quoted in "Prayer Quotes," *HopeFaithPrayer.com*; http://hopefaithprayer.com/prayernew/prayer-quotes/ (accessed February 21, 2012).

Chapter 2: A Devotional Prayer Lifestyle

1. Murray M'Cheyene, quoted in "Christian Prayer Quotes;" http://www.christian-prayer-quotes.christian-attorney.net/ (accessed February 21, 2012).

2. William Carey, quoted in Ibid.

3. *American Heritage Dictionary*, s.v. "Manifest"; http://www.answers.com/topic/manifest (accessed February 22, 2012).

Chapter 3: Salvation Is Wonderful...But There's More!

1. Oral Roberts, *Unleashing the Power of Praying in the Spirit* (Tulsa, OK: Harrison House, 1993), 139.

Chapter 4: Learning to Fast and Pray

1. Andrew Murray, quoted in "Christian Prayer Quotes"; http://www.christian-prayer-quotes.christian-attorney.net/ (accessed February 22, 2012).

Chapter 5: Revival Fires

1. Smith Wigglesworth, *Smith Wigglesworth on Spiritual Gifts* (New Kensington, PA: Whittaker House, 2002), 16.

Chapter 6: "I Want You to Build a Place"

1. E.M. Bounds, quoted in "Christian Prayer Quotes"; http://www.christian-prayer-quotes.christian-attorney.net/ (accessed February 22, 2012).

Chapter 7: Our Commitment Is Tested

1. Andrew Murray, quoted in "Christian Prayer Quotes"; http://www.christian-prayer-quotes.christian-attorney.net/ (accessed February 22, 2012).

Chapter 8: The Vision Is Growing

1. J. Hudson Taylor, quoted in "Christian Prayer Quotes"; http://www.christian-prayer-quotes.christian-attorney.net/ (accessed February 22, 2012).

2. Robert Thom, *The New Wine is Better,* CD series, available at http://www.robynthomrodgers.com/index-3.html (accessed February 22, 2012).

Chapter 9: Moving Forward…Again

1. R.A. Torrey, quoted in "Christian Prayer Quotes"; http://www.christian-prayer-quotes.christian-attorney.net/ (accessed February 23, 2012).

Chapter 10: Seeking God for Miracles

1. Andrew Murray, quoted in "Christian Prayer Quotes"; http://www.christian-prayer-quotes.christian-attorney.net/ (accessed February 23, 2012).

2. For more about Arthur Burt and his ministry, visit http://arthur-burt.com/.

3. *Blue Letter Bible*, s.v. "Semeion" (Strong's Greek #4592); http://www.blueletterbible.org/lang/lexicon/lexicon.cfm?Strongs=G4592andt=KJV (accessed February 23, 2012).

Chapter 11: Cultivating a Worshipping Heart

1. E.M. Bounds, quoted in "Christian Prayer Quotes"; http://www.christian-prayer-quotes.christian-attorney.net/ (accessed February 23, 2012).

2. A.B. Simpson, *Days of Heaven on Earth,* (Camp Hill, PA: Christian Publications, 1984).

Chapter 12: Surprised by the Holy Spirit

1. A.T. Pierson, quoted in J. Edwin Orr, "Prayer and Revival," *JEdwinOrr.com;* http://www.jedwinorr.com/prayer_revival.htm (accessed February 23, 2012).

Chapter 13: Learning to Pray Corporately

1. Samuel Chadwick, quoted in "Christian Prayer Quotes"; http://www.christian-prayer-quotes.christian-attorney.net/ (accessed February 23, 2012).

2. Sue Curran, *The Praying Church* (Shippensburg, PA: Destiny Image, 2007).

3. Charles Finney, quoted in *Ibid.*

4. Charles G. Finney, *Lectures on Revival* (Minneapolis, MN: Bethany House, 1989), 54.

5. Dr. Fuchsia Pickett, *Walking in the Anointing of the Holy Spirit, Book II* (Lake Mary, FL: Charisma House, 2004), 66.

Chapter 14: The Power of Agreement

1. Mahesh Chavda, *The Hidden Power of Prayer and Fasting* (Shippensburg, PA: Destiny Image, 2007), 132.

2. Sue Curran, *The Praying Church* (Lake Mary, FL: Creation House, 1987, 2001), 40.

Chapter 15: The Holy Spirit Is a Divine Person

1. Oswald Chambers, quoted in "Christian Prayer Quotes"; http://www.christian-prayer-quotes.christian-attorney.net/ (accessed February 23, 2012).

2. Fuchsia Pickett, *Stones of Remembrance* (Lake Mary, FL: Charisma House, 1998).

3. Fuchsia Pickett, *Understanding the Personality of the Holy Spirit, Book I* (Lake Mary, FL: Charisma House, 2004), 79-110.

Chapter 16: Birthing God's Purposes Through Prayer

1. Kenneth E. Hagin, *The Art of Intercession* (Tulsa, OK: Faith Library, 1980).

2. Myles Munroe, *Understanding the Purpose and Priority of Prayer* (New Kensington, PA: Whittaker House, 2002), 16.

3. "Kenneth Meshoe," *Who's Who Southern Africa*; http://www.who-swhosa.co.za/kenneth-meshoe-943 (accessed February 23, 2012).

Chapter 17: Surprised by Revival in New Zealand

1. E.M. Bounds, quoted in "Christian Prayer Quotes"; http://www.christian-prayer-quotes.christian-attorney.net/ (accessed February 23, 2012).

Chapter 18: Seeking His Presence—Anywhere

1. Andrew A. Bonar, quoted in "Christian Prayer Quotes"; http://www.christian-prayer-quotes.christian-attorney.net/ (accessed February 23, 2012).

2. One such pastor is Sunday Adelaja, pastor of the Embassy of the Blessed Kingdom of God for all Nations. Visit their website for

more information: www.godembassy.org/en/pastor.php (accessed February 23, 2012).

Chapter 19: Learning to Pray Strategically

1. E.M. Bounds, quoted in "Christian Prayer Quotes"; http://www.christian-prayer-quotes.christian-attorney.net/ (accessed February 24, 2012).

2. Oswald Chambers, quoted in Ibid.

3. Sue Curran, *Prayer in Another Dimension* (Shippensburg, PA: Destiny Image Publishers, 2007).

4. "Archbishop Nicolas Duncan-Williams," *Duncan-Williams Ministries;* http://www.duncanwilliamsministry.com/bishop.html (accessed February 24, 2012)

5. Bishop Bart Pierce, pastor of Rock City Church, Baltimore, Maryland; http://www.rockcitychurch.com (accessed February 24, 2012).

6. Bishop Nicolas Duncan-Williams, quoted in Sue Curran, *Prayer in Another Dimension* (Shippensburg, PA: Destiny Image Publishers, 2007), 95.

7. *Vine's Expository Dictionary of New Testament Words,* s.v. "Anoint, Anointing (Unction)"; http://www.blueletterbible.org/Search/Dictionary/viewTopic.cfm?type=getTopicandTopic=Anoint%2C+AnointingandDictID=9#Vines (accessed February 24, 2012).

8. Sue Curran, *Prayer in Another Dimension,* 107.

Chapter 20: To Mozambique With Love

1. Charles H. Spurgeon, quoted in "Christian Prayer Quotes"; http://www.christian-prayer-quotes.christian-attorney.net/ (accessed February 24, 2012).

2. Rolland Baker, "About Us," *Iris Ministries*; http://www.irismin. org/about (accessed February 24, 2012).

3. "About Iris," *Iris Ministries*; http://www.irismin.org/home (accessed February 24, 2012).

4. Rolland and Heidi Baker, "Pressing on to the Best Yet," newsletter, *Iris Ministries* (February 27, 2010); http://www.irismin.org/news/newsletters/view/pressing-on-to-the-best-yet (accessed February 24, 2012).

5. Rolland Baker, "Enjoying Our God," newsletter, *Iris Ministries* (May 8, 2010); http://www.irismin.org/news/newsletters/view/enjoying-our-god (accessed February 24, 2012).

Chapter 21: Learning Through Suffering

1. E.M. Bounds, quoted in "Christian Prayer Quotes"; http://www.christian-prayer-quotes.christian-attorney.net/ (accessed February 24, 2012).

2. John Follette, *Golden Grain* (Asheville, NC: Follette Books, 1985), 97.

3. Mary Stevenson, "Footprints in the Sand," http://www.footprints-inthe-sand.com/index.php?page=Poem/Poem.php (accessed February 24, 2012).

4. "Emerson and Ana Mendez Ferrell," *Ambassador's Ministries*; http://www.ambasmin.org/en/MinistryAnaEmerson.html (accessed February 24, 2012).

5. Mel Tari and Cliff Dudley, *Like a Mighty Wind* (Green Forest, AR: New Leaf Press, 1971).

Chapter 22: More Lessons in Healing

1. E.M. Bounds, quoted in "Christian Prayer Quotes"; http://www.christian-prayer-quotes.christian-attorney.net/ (accessed February 24, 2012).

2. For more information on Norvel Hayes Ministries, visit their website: http://www.nhm.cc/.

3. "Revival History," *Bay of the Holy Spirit Revival*; http://bayoftheholyspiritrevival.com/about.php (accessed February 24, 2012).

Chapter 23: School Isn't Out Yet

1. E.M. Bounds, quoted in "Christian Prayer Quotes"; http://www.christian-prayer-quotes.christian-attorney.net/ (accessed February 24, 2012).

2. Thomas Hooker, quoted in Ibid.

3. Smith Wigglesworth, quoted in *Women of Destiny Bible* (Nashville, TN: Thomas Nelson, 2000), 691.

4. "Pastor Delia Knox," *Living Word Christian Center International Ministries*; http://www.lwccim.com/bio_pastordelia.html (accessed February 24, 2012).

5. Rolland Baker, "Enjoying Our God," newsletter, *Iris Ministries* (May 8, 2010); http://www.irismin.org/news/newsletters/view/enjoying-our-god (accessed February 24, 2012).

6. *Blue Letter Bible*, s.v. "Mashak" (Strong's Hebrew #4900); http://www.blueletterbible.org/lang/lexicon/lexicon.cfm?Strongs=H4900andt=KJV (accessed February 24, 2012).

7. *Blue Letter Bible*, s.v. "Paraklesis" (Strong's Greek #3874); http://www.blueletterbible.org/lang/lexicon/lexicon.cfm?Strongs=G3874andt=KJV (accessed February 24, 2012).

Appendix A: Biblical Praise Expressions

1. Vivien Hibbert, *Prophetic Worship* (Dallas, TX: Cuington Press, 1999), 66-69.

Appendix B: Hindrances to Corporate Prayer

1. Sue Curran, *The Praying Church* (Lake Mary, FL: Creation House, 1987, 2001).

Appendix C: The Seven Offices of the Holy Spirit

1. Fuchsia T. Pickett, *Walking in the Anointing of the Holy Spirit* (Lake Mary, FL: Charisma House, 2004), 43-75.

Appendix D: Great Awakenings in Our Nation

1. Roberts Liardon, *The Azusa Street Revival* (Shippensburg, PA: Destiny Image, 2006), 35-36.

2. *Ibid.*, 39.

3. *Ibid.*, 46.

4. "Second Great Awakening: Religious revival movement had profound impact in U.S.," *America.gov Archive* (April 5, 2008); http://www.america.gov/st/educ-english/2008/April/200804071135I9eaifas0.3545038.html (accessed February 25, 2012).

RECOMMENDED READING

Bounds, E.M.
Power Through Prayer. Grand Rapids, MI: Zondervan Publishing House, 1987.
The Best of E.M. Bounds on Prayer. Grand Rapids, MI: Baker Book House, 1987.

Carre, Captain E.G.
Praying Hyde. North Brunswick, NJ: Bridge-Logos Publishers, 1982.

Cho, Paul Yonggi.
Prayer: Key to Revival. Dallas, TX: Word Books, 1984.

Cornwall, Judson.
Praying the Scriptures. Lake Mary, FL: Creation House, 1988.

Curran, Sue.
Prayer in Another Dimension. Shippensburg, PA: Destiny Image, 2007.
The Praying Church. Lake Mary, FL: Creation House, 2004.

Facius, Johannes.
The Powerhouse of God. Kent, England: Sovereign World, 1995.

Goll, Jim W.
The Lost Art of Intercession. Shippensburg, PA: Revival Press, 1997.

Grubb, Norman.
Rees Howells, Intercessor. 3rd Edition. Fort Washington, PA: Christian Literature Crusade, 1983.

Hagin, Kenneth E.
The Art of Intercession. Tulsa, OK: Faith Library Publications, 1981.

Liardon, Roberts.
John G. Lake. Tulsa, OK: Albury Publishing, 1998.
Smith Wigglesworth. Tulsa, OK: Albury Publishing, 1996.

Lindsay, Gordon.
Prayer that Moves Mountains. Dallas, TX: Christ for the Nations, 1994.

MacIntyre, David M.
The Hidden Life of Prayer. Houston, TX: Christian Focus Publications, 1989.

Mueller, George.
Answers to Prayer. Chicago, IL: Moody Press, 1984.

Murray, Andrew.
The Believer's School of Prayer. Bloomington, MN: Bethany, 1998.
The Ministry of Intercessory Prayer. Bloomington, MN: Bethany, 1998.
With Christ in the School of Prayer. Reprint. Grand Rapids, MI: Zondervan, 1983.

Sheets, Dutch.
Intercessory Prayer. Ventura, CA: Regal Books, 1996.

Torrey, R.A.
The Power of Prayer. Grand Rapids, MI: Zondervan, 1971.

ABOUT DR. SUE CURRAN

Dr. Sue Curran, along with her husband John, is the founder and pastor of Shekinah Church in Blountville, Tennessee. Shekinah hosts annual conferences for leadership development and prayer and worship summits for the Body of Christ. Their local church has grown in influence around the world through the work of a praying and worshiping leadership and congregation. As a result, Dr. Curran has been propelled into a strong teaching and apostolic ministry that focuses on strategic prayer and addresses root causes of ineffectiveness in prayer.

Dr. Curran holds both Master and Doctor of Divinity degrees from Christian Life School of Theology and is an adjunct professor for Christian Life Educator's Network. She is an internationally recognized conference speaker and an effective minister in areas of prayer, spiritual freedom and revival.

From the outset of her teaching ministry, authentic revival has accompanied Dr. Curran's presentation of the full gospel in its simplicity. Her ministry has extended to all continents, crossing many cultural and ethnic boundaries with the same revival impact.

The author of two other powerful books on prayer, Dr. Curran teaches biblical principles that contrast the reserved prayer posture of the Western church with the bold, fervent, effective prayers of Christians in other nations. *Define Your Destiny Through Prayer* reveals how

Shekinah, an international ministry, came from nothing to a ministry with worldwide influence. The Holy Spirit taught her to pray out of the necessity of learning how to touch God for miracles of every kind to see the work established.

OTHER BOOKS BY DR. SUE CURRAN

Freer than You Ever Dreamed

The Praying Church

The Forgiving Church

I Saw Satan Fall Like Lightning

Prayer in Another Dimension

Intensive courses on DVD are available for college credit or audit through Christian Life School of Theology on the following subjects:

The Praying Church

The Forgiving Church

Freer Than You Ever Dreamed

Prayer in Another Dimension

Define Your Destiny Through Prayer

A complete list of books, CDs and DVDs are available from:

Shekinah Church
394 Glory Rd.
Blountville, TN 37617

423-323-2242

www.shekinah.net

For speaking engagements and itinerary please visit:
www.suecurran.com.